Ceramic Art Tile
for the home

DeBorah Goletz

Schiffer Publishing Ltd

4880 Lower Valley Road, Atglen, PA 19310 USA

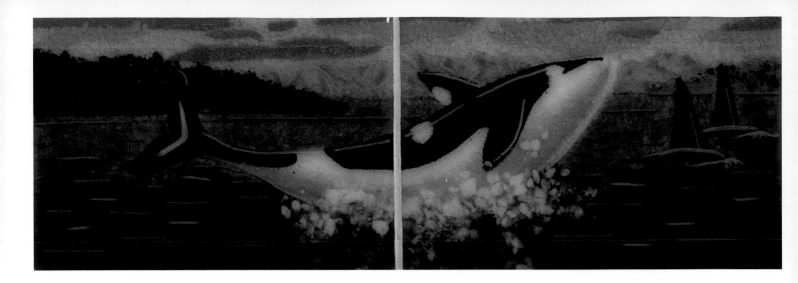

Back cover: DeBorah Goletz surrounded by freshly made tile.
Photograph by Kristie Glah Fairchild

Title Page: Michelle Griffoul, Michelle Griffoul Studios, *Flying Fish*
staircase. *Photograph by Brian Fritz Photography.*

Library of Congress Cataloging-in-Publication Data

Goletz, DeBorah.
Ceramic art tile for your home / by DeBorah Goletz.
p. cm.
ISBN 0-7643-1297-9
1. Tiles in interior decoration. I. Title.
NK2115.5. T54 G65 2001
747'9.--dc21
00-013252

Copyright © 2001 by DeBorah Goletz

Designed by Bonnie M. Hensley
Cover design by Bruce M. Waters
Type set in Papyrus LET/Humanist 521

ISBN: 0-7643-1297-9
Printed in China

Published by Schiffer Publishing Ltd.
4880 Lower Valley Road
Atglen, PA 19310
Phone: (610) 593-1777; Fax: (610) 593-2002
E-mail: Schifferbk@aol.com
Please visit our web site catalog at
www.schifferbooks.com

This book may be purchased from the publisher.
Include $3.95 for shipping.
Please try your bookstore first.
We are always looking for people to write books on new and related subjects.
If you have an idea for a book please contact us at the above address.
You may write for a free catalog.

In Europe, Schiffer books are distributed by
Bushwood Books
6 Marksbury Avenue
Kew Gardens
Surrey TW9 4JF England
Phone: 44 (0) 20-8392-8585; Fax: 44 (0) 20-8392-9876
E-mail: Bushwd@aol.com
Free postage in the UK. Europe: air mail at cost.

Dedication

To Mom and Dad, for believing in my dreams, and Eric
and Alex, for sharing them

Some tile makers, like myself, started as potters who became interested in tile. others came to tile from unrelated fields. The pages of this book are filled with hundreds of photographs of breathtaking tilework and "Meet the Artist" segments, offering you the opportunity to get to know some of the tile makers themselves. Each artist has a unique set of circumstances which led them to tile, and to the designs they create.

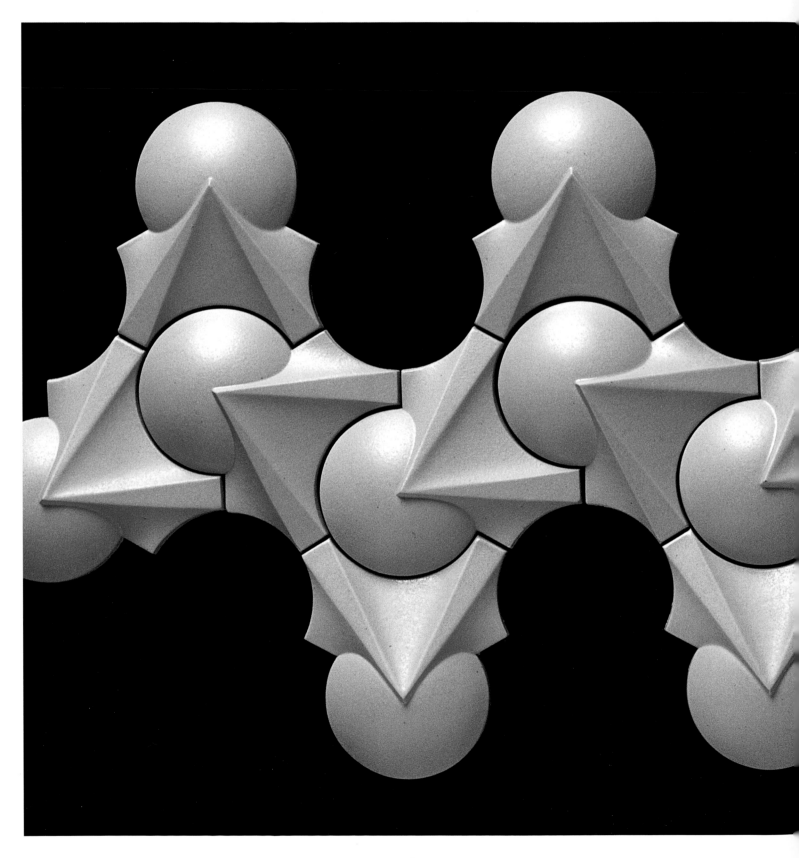

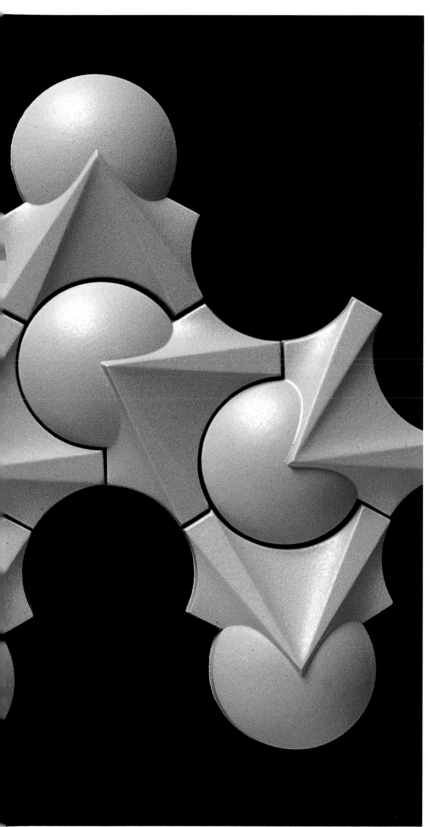

Table of Contents

Foreword
by Frank Giorgini

There is something so pleasing about walking into a room decorated with handmade art tile. Patterns, images and shapes created by the mind and hands of an artist are frozen in time on the tile surface, creating an environment that is both comforting and pleasurable. Ceramic tile are formed from the earth and can command a formidable presence with their beauty and permanence. The allure of art tile is timeless.

I have been involved in tile making and teaching handmade tile design for over twenty years. My background in sculpture and industrial design combined with my passion for clay enables me to pursue a career as a tile artist and educator. DeBorah Goletz and I worked together at Parsons School of Design in New York City for many years, becoming best of friends, and still are. During that period I authored my book, *Handmade Tiles* (Lark Books, 1994) and now I am honored to contribute to DeBorah's book.

The tile class at Parsons became a center for aspiring tile artists from New York and around the country. Making handmade tile was fast becoming the most popular form of ceramic expression and the classes were always full. Several students went on to start their own art tile businesses. Some, including Elizabeth Grajales, DeBorah, and I brought our talents to the level of designing and producing art tile for public art projects, including the New York City subway system. But the majority of students were taking the course to make tile of their own creation for their own homes and apartments. Whether they completed these projects or not, they gained a new appreciation for the art of handmade tile.

Not everyone will ever get to make a tile, but everyone can appreciate them. DeBorah has created a visually exciting and most informative resource for all who wish to enhance their homes and their lives with the enduring beauty of handmade artisan tile. Tile on!

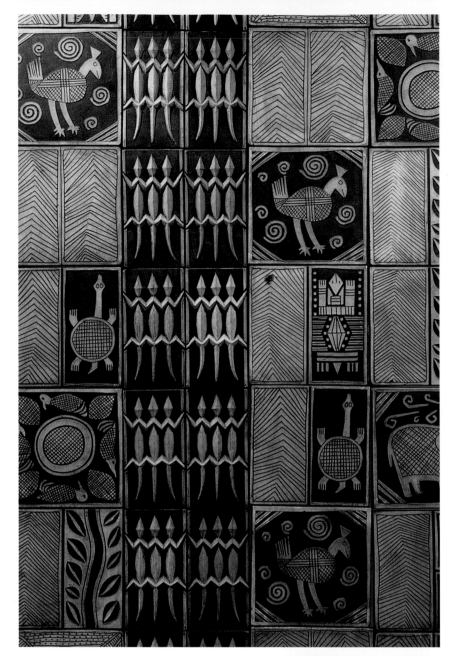

Frank Giorgini, Giorgini Studio, *Afro Tiles*, 12" x 12" relief tile. *Photograph by Bobby Hansson*

Diane Winters, Winters Tileworks, texured border tile and thin liners frame a 6" x 6" *Magnolia B* tile.

DeBorah Goletz, *Ivy,* sample relief tile developed for John McIntire Library project.

Elizabeth Grajales, *Garden Series* relief tile, 18" x 12".

Lynda Curtis, L. Curtis Designs, *Edo Kan'ei* handpainted mural, China Grill Restaurant, Miami Beach, FL. *Photograph by Ed Wolkis*

Introduction

As a potter and tile maker I am more comfortable expressing ideas through clay than words. I'm fortunate to have my mural work in the public realm and have enjoyed the attention that comes with that privilege. I first learned how to make tile in 1989 from Frank Giorgini at Parsons School of Design, where we both worked for more than ten years. Membership in the Tile Heritage Foundation, many experiences with tile artists, and many wonderful books on the subject of art tile expanded my technical and historical knowledge of the craft. But when approached by Schiffer Publishing to write this book, I wondered how to convey my passion for tile to others.

The answer came through conversations I have had with dozens of talented tile artisans throughout the country and seeing the diverse and exciting range of work they produce. Tile studios are cropping up in every state. Some are large and well-equipped, others operate from home garages. But designers and tile showroom experts agree that the range and quality of these artisans' tile make them the most exciting products on the market. This book is a celebration of the tile work being made by hand, by artists in the U.S.A. today. Here is an opportunity to feast your eyes upon the exquisite, the humorous, the unorthodox, and the classic. It's all here—something for every taste, every lifestyle. And here is a chance to learn about the artists themselves and how designers and architects are finding new ways to use this rich art form.

Judy Glasser, stoneware mural, carved relief tile, 21" x 33 1/2". *Photograph by George Erml*

Linda Ellett, L'esperance Tile Works, relief tile. The bird design was influenced by shamanic ivory carvings of the Inuit Indians. 3" x 6 1/2"

Paul Zelenka, Unicorn Studio, *Griffin*, Medieval series, 6" x 6".

Rosalyn Tyge, Tyge Tile/Art, art deco wall piece, 17" x 30".
Photograph by John Robert Williams

Adriana Baler, Adriana Baler Tiles, relief tile.

Phil Raskin, North Prairie Tileworks, relief tile with handpainted glaze.

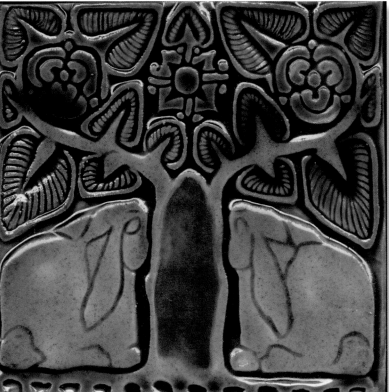

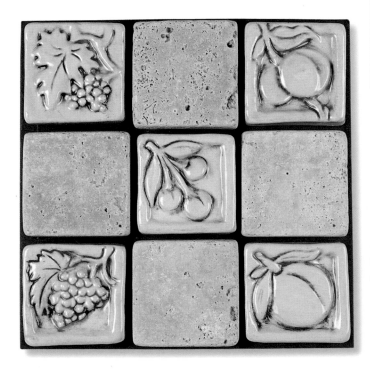

Linda Shields, Atherton Tile Company, *Antique Fruit* insert tile, 1 3/4" x 1 3/4" each. *Photograph by Don Roper Photography*

Steven and Susan Kemenyffy, *A Study in Bright*, 28" x 24" raku wall form. *Photograph by Ed Bernik Photography.*

Chapter One

Tile Fever

According to Robert Daniels, Executive Director of the Tile Council of America, the US tile market has grown steadily over the last ten years, and by as much as 14% in each of the last five years. The market for art tile is estimated to be growing even faster. Currently, Americans purchase approximately six square feet of tile per year per person. Compare that to Portugal, Spain, Italy, and China, where domestic tile consumption is 30 to 40 square feet per year per person, and where tile is also manufactured for export. The American tile industry holds the potential to reach these market levels as more and more people look to add the value, permanence, and beauty of tile to their home. And increasingly, art tile is being chosen as a personal, artistic alternative to the ubiquitous commercial tile that swathes the kitchens and baths of so many homes in this country.

Nancy Epstein, founder and President of Artistic Tile Showrooms, notes that Americans are travelling more, and are becoming more aware of how tile is used throughout the rest of the world. As a result, they are inclined to use more tile in their homes and place greater value on it. Kitchens, bathrooms, and entryways are no longer the only rooms that sport tile. Busy lifestyles make the durability and easy maintenance of ceramic surfaces more appreciated than ever.

Ceramic tile responds slowly to temperature change, making it feel cool to the touch. This, and the fact that it is well suited for installation directly on concrete slab, makes it an ideal floor (and wall) covering in warm climates. In regions where the winters are cold, wood and carpeting have been the traditional choices for flooring. But thanks to new technologies, tile is now used with energy efficient in-floor heating systems in these regions. More and more new homeowners are experiencing the delightful sensation of warm tile underfoot as they step out of bed or from the shower.

Ceramic tile is available in every price range. Art tile, however, has been considered a high-end product, and subject to the ups and downs of the economy. The current economic climate has certainly contributed to the recent boom in building and remodelling. Art tile is meeting the increasing desire for original home decor with both traditional and innovative designs.

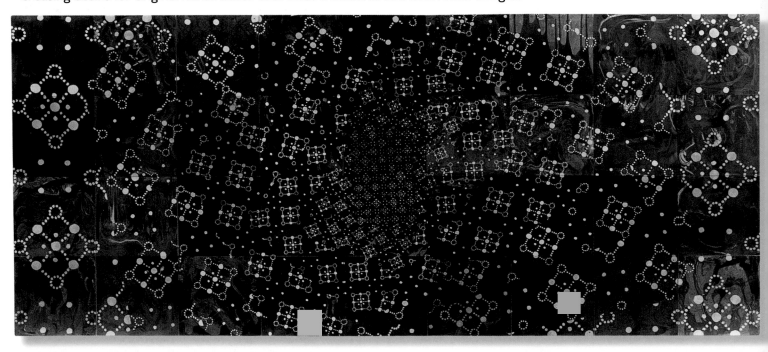

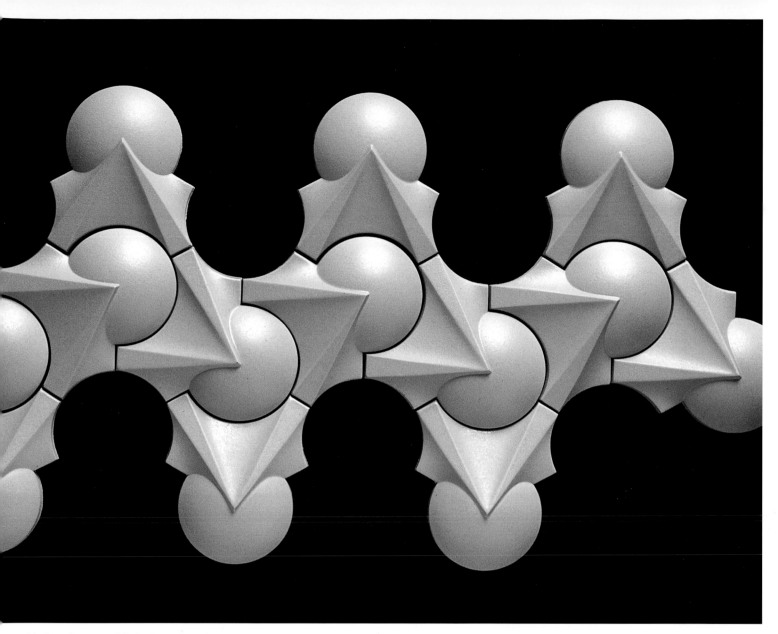

Neilsen Amon and Ruby Levesque, Amon Art Tile, *Mars Cluster* relief tile, each approximately 3 1/2" x 4". *Photograph by Herman Estevez*

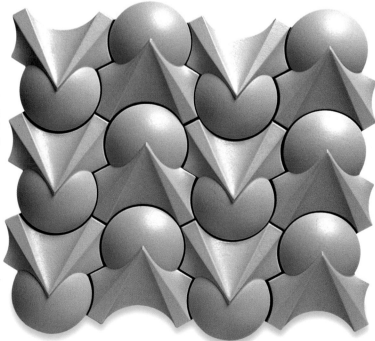

Neilsen Amon and Ruby Levesque, Amon Art Tile, *Mars Cluster* relief tile. *Photograph by Herman Estevez*

Opposite page: Frank Bosco, *Composition #3*, modified encaustic technique tile, 78" x 175 1/2". *Photograph by Les Helmers*

Anne & Edward Nocera, Nocera Art Tile Company, *Table with Koi and Lily Pads*, 32" x 32", handpainted tile. *Photograph by Edward Nocera*

Natalie Surving, Surving Studios, *Iguana Mural*, composed of 15 individual tile, 6" x 6" each.

Kim Gore, Kim Gore Hand-Sculpted Tile Co., *Medallion,* carved relief tile, 4" x 4". *Photograph by Peter Smith*

Kim Gore, Kim Gore Hand-Sculpted Tile Co., medallion relief tile set on diagonal with field tile. *Photograph by Peter Smith*

Michelle Griffoul, Michelle Griffoul Studios,
Sea Creature Shower, ceramic mosaic tile.
Photograph by Peter Malinowski

Michelle Griffoul, Michelle Griffoul
Studios, *Palm Border* backsplash, ceramic
mosaic tile. *Photograph by Peter
Malinowski*

Chapter Two

Tile Making in the U.S.

The manufacture of art tile in this country began around 1875. Prior to this, aside from a few potters making limited quantities of handmade tile, only wealthy Americans could afford imported tile from Europe.

Potteries and tile factories rose up in areas of the country where suitable clay was readily available. The first of these were located in Massachusetts, New York, New Jersey, Pennsylvania, and Ohio. Several of these factories employed immigrant tile craftsmen from Europe who brought technical information with them to the States. Economic growth following the civil war spurred an interest in home decor, and tile soon became a key element of Victorian design. J. & J.G. Low Art Tile Works, Moravian Pottery & Tile Works, Pewabic Pottery and Batchelder Tile Company are just a few of the early tile producers whose designs are re-produced today.

American-made tile was soon being used in government buildings, opera houses, financial institutions, and places where heavy traffic required the durability of a ceramic surface. But the American tile industry began to serve more than just this strictly functional need. Art tile was being produced for decorative uses such as fireplace surrounds, architectural elements, and murals. Designs proliferated as tile craftsmen exploited the medium's facility for self expression. And as the public's desire for art tile increased, tile craftsmen moved across the country from one factory to another where they would produce similar (and sometimes identical) designs.

These designs ranged from the simple to the very elaborate and depicted all aspects of life and fantasy. Art Deco and classical figures, rural settings, geometric patterns, portraits, floral images, and historic scenes all found themselves immortalized in American art tile. Glazes were developed with pale translucent colors to highlight carved tile. Other tile were unglazed, or bathed in stony matte glazes of rich color. By around 1910, tile factories had reached the west coast where the *California style* of tile developed, which used brighter, more intensely colored glazes and extravagant floral patterns.

The staid Victorian designs of commercial imported tile could no longer compete with this flamboyant new domestic art form. By the turn of the twentieth century, Americans had developed a love affair with art tile which would last for the next 30 years. They used it on floors and walls, fireplaces and fountains, as architectural elements on buildings and homes, and displayed it as decorative *objects d'arte*. The lavish art tile installed in the New York City subway system became famous for its graphic identification of each station for immigrant riders who did not yet read English.

But the tile factories were dependant upon a healthy economy, and the Depression took its toll on the industry. By the mid-1930s many of the factories had closed. American art tile was no longer produced on a large scale.

In the late 1940s a post-World War II boom in home construction created a tremendous market for mass-produced tile. Art tile was all but forgotten as standardized sanitary tile took over the industry. A decade later, when the age of Modernism created a desire for industrial products, home designers embraced the standard white "four by four's". Commercial tile so pervaded the market place that by 1960 every small town in America sported a tile store featuring standardized lines of tile in white, pastels, harvest gold and olive green.

It wasn't until the 1960s that a few potters began to make art tile again in the U.S. Their earthy tones were in sharp contrast to the white and pastel commercial tile products. High-end tile showrooms began to spring up in urban centers. These shops primarily featured imported tile from

Europe and Asia. More and more American tile makers emerged, particularly in the past ten years. In fact, now the U.S. boasts the broadest range of tile designs, and the richest glaze choices available. There is a renaissance going on in the American art tile industry which is blossoming in small domestic potteries and tileworks. Fueled by readily available technical information and materials (not to mention talent) American tile makers are producing the most interesting varieties of art tile in the world market.

Delia Tapp and Marie Glasse Tapp, Tile Restorations Center, fireplace with reproduction Batchelder tile. Ernest Allen Batchelder founded the Batchelder Tile Company in Pasadena, California in 1909. It was re-named Batchelder & Brown in 1912, and Batchelder & Wilson in 1920. The company was best known for relief tile, which it produced until closing in 1932. *Photograph by Don Mason.*

Delia Tapp and Marie Glasse Tapp, Tile Restorations Center, detail, fireplace with reproduction Batchelder tile, *photograph by Don Mason.*

Linda Ellett, L'esperance Tile Works, reproduction of original tile by Arthur Osborne, who was the top designer for the J.G. Low Tile Company. J. & J.G. Low Art Tile Works, later called the J.G. & J.F. Low Art Tile Works, operated in Chelsea, Massachusetts from 1877 to 1902. This tile is approximately 5" x 7".

Delia Tapp and Marie Glasse Tapp, Tile Restoration Center, reproduction of Batchelder carved relief tile. Pine Cones, center tile is 6" x 6", trim tile is 2" x 6", corner tile is 2" x 2".

Delia Tapp and Marie Glasse Tapp, Tile Restoration Center,
Reproduction of Batchelder relief tile, 12" x 12"

Moravian Tile Works has been in existence on the same location in Doylestown, Pennsylvania since 1912, founded by Henry Mercer. This is an original Moravian tile design which is still being made today at the tile works.

Moravian Tile Works

Linda Ellett, L'esperance Tile Works, Reproduction of J.G. Low border tile surrounds classical Angel & Griffin tile. Approximately 11" x 13".

Linda Ellett, L'esperance Tile Works, Reproduction of J.G. Low border tile surrounds reproduction *Daylily* panel from American Encaustic Tile Company (AET). AET operated in Zanesville, Ohio from 1875 to 1935. Approximately 28" x 10".

Nancy Chevalier-Guido, fireplace surround designed by Wendy Sample, fabricated by Nancy Chevalier-Guido (colored tile is salvaged, antique Pewabic tile). Pewabic Pottery and Tile Works has been in operation in Detroit, Michigan since 1903. *Photograph by Bruce Harkness*

Chapter Three

What Defines Art Tile?

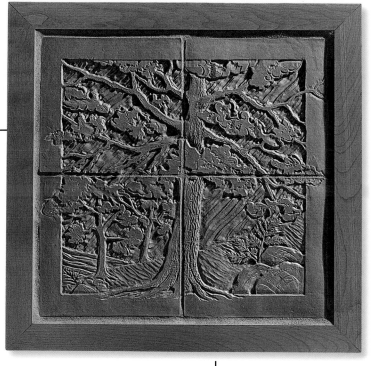

Steve de Perrot, Pots by de Perrot, *Oak Tree*, carved relief tile, 22" x 22". *Photograph by Larry Lefever*

Broadly defined, art tile, (also called handmade tile and artisan tile) is tile which is repeatedly touched by human hands during its fabrication. The term "fabrication" is preferred over the term "manufacture" because of the latter's reference to machine-made products. There are several different types of art tile, each defined by its fabrication process. *Handpainted tile* features designs which are painted and glazed by hand—though the tile themselves are not necessarily formed by hand. Some handpainted tile makers use machine-made blanks, while others use handmade tile upon which to paint their designs. *Cut tile* are cut from rolled-out sheets of clay, often using *tile cutters* (like cookie cutters). *Relief tile* are carved or formed by hand, then cast in plaster to create forms known as *molds* which enable multiples of the tile to be fabricated. *One-of-a-kind* tile are usually formed and glazed without molds and without the intention of being reproduced. An example of a one-of-a-kind tile might be one in which leaves or flowers are pressed into the tile's surface to create a design. Even if the process is repeated, each tile bears the imprint of different leaves. Another process that yields one-of-a-kind tile is *raku firing* (described later in this chapter) which creates unique glaze effects upon each tile. *Encaustic* and *inlaid* tile are made with several clays of various colors. A single-colored tile is impressed or incised to form recesses which are filled with clays of contrasting color. These make durable flooring because the color is integral to the tile itself, and cannot wear off the surface. *Sgraffiato* tile also uses layers of clay. The design is scratched into the surface layer to reveal the contrasting layer below. *Raised line* tile, as the name implies, features a thin raised (embossed) line drawing or pattern which is sometimes used to keep multiple glaze colors separated from each other.

Ceramic tile are made with *fire clay*. Fire clay requires exposure to extreme heat in a kiln to become hard (vitreous). Particular types of fire clay are referred to as *clay bodies*. The chemical components vary in each clay body, but the primary ingredients are always alumina and silica (a form of glass, also known as flint). *Terra-cotta* clay bodies and many *stoneware* clay bodies also contain iron, which gives them their characteristic red or brown color. *Porcelain* and other white clay bodies do not contain iron.

Plastic clay is the type of clay that most people are familiar with. This clay is soft and malleable. Plastic clay can be pressed into tile molds, rolled out into sheets like dough, cut with cutters, or modelled into relief tile. Many tile artists use plastic clay to form tile. The use of plastic clay in the forming process is what gives art tile slightly softer edges than commercial tile which is most often formed with clay dust.

Clay dust, as the name indicates, is dry or nearly dry powdered clay. Industry uses clay dust (instead of plastic clay) to manufacture tile. It is compressed, with powerful hydraulic machines, into molds. The resultant tile is instantly dry and ready to be fired.

Slip is clay in liquid form, which is used to make pottery and other objects from plaster molds. Slip is poured into a mold, allowed to harden on the inner surface of the mold (the mold draws water from the clay) then released from the mold. Slip is also used as a decorating medium when it is poured or brushed onto clay.

When plastic clay is allowed to dry a bit, it passes through a stage called *leather hard*. In this stage the clay is firm to the touch, but it still contains moisture—the consistency is similar to a block of cheese. When it is leather hard, clay can be cut, carved or incised leaving sharp, clean edges difficult to achieve when the clay is soft. This stage is particularly useful for carving and creating inlay designs.

When clay dries, water evaporates from between the molecules in it which are thus drawn closer together. This drying creates *shrinkage* (the tile literally shrinks as it dries). Different clay bodies shrink at different rates. Plastic clay may also have a tendency to warp during this process, due to uneven drying conditions (for instance, if the top surface of a tile dries (and shrinks) faster than the bottom surface). Plastic clay also has a memory. The clay's plate-like molecules configure themselves during modelling and molding as well as with subsequent handling. If a tile maker is not careful and mis-handles a tile when it is soft, (prior to leather hard) it will bend. Even if the tile is immediately re-shaped, the bend may re-appear during drying or firing (if the molecules return to their former position). Controlling the drying, shrinking and warping of plastic clay is the tile maker's prime objective during tile fabrication. Temperature and humidity play critical roles in determining the success of the fabrication process.

In its fully dry state the clay is referred to as *bone dry,* or *greenware*. Bone dry clay looks and feels absolutely dry, though water (H_2O) is still present in it. That's because H_2O is chemically combined in the molecular structure of the clay itself. During firing, the clay is warmed slowly, allowing the chemically combined H_2O to be released as steam. If the steam is released too quickly as a result of rapidly increasing temperature, the tile may crack or burst.

Clay continues to shrink during the *firing* process, which is accomplished in a *kiln* (ceramic oven) designed to reach high temperatures. During the firing, the molecular components of the clay change into an irreversible, hardened, vitrified state. Different clay bodies require different firing temperatures. Generally, terra-cotta is referred to as a *low-fire clay* and is fired to between 1800° and 1950° Fahrenheit (F). Stonewares are *mid-range* or *high-fire clays* which are fired to 2100°F (mid-range) or up to 2300°F (high fire). Porcelain is usually high fired (to 2300°F and above). The level of vitrification, or hardness of a tile, depends upon how high (hot) it is fired. Terra-cotta, being a low-fire clay, remains porous (low vitrification) after firing and requires a glaze or sealant to keep it from absorbing water. Stoneware and porcelain tile are fired hotter, becoming more vitrified, which makes them more water resistant, with or without glaze.

Tile which is to be used outdoors in freezing climates must have a water absorption level below 3% (of the weight of the fired tile) to be classified as *frost-proof*. Tile artists who create murals and outdoor tile that is exposed to these conditions must know these standards when selecting a clay body. Clay distributors publish the shrinkage and absorption rates of the clay bodies they sell. Clay artists who process their own clay body must conduct tests to check shrinkage and absorption rates.

Much art tile is fired twice. The first is a low temperature (approximately 1800° F) firing without glaze. This is called a *bisque* or *biscuit firing*. After this firing, tile is hard but still porous. These are useful qualities during application of glaze. Once glaze is applied, a second firing is accomplished (to a higher temperature for stoneware and porcelain tile).

Some tile are left unglazed, exposing the raw clay for an earthy stone-like finish. But most ceramic tile are glazed fully or in part. *Glaze* is a glass shell fused to the surface of a tile. Glaze can be transparent, opaque, shiny or matte and can be formulated in every color imaginable. It is composed of several elements which fall into three basic components: 1) silica (found in clay bodies), 2) alumina (also found in clay bodies), and a flux (which lowers the melting temperature of the silica glass). Commonly used fluxes include barium, calcium, lithium, magnesium, potassium, sodium and zinc. Lead is a flux which was commonly used by early tile makers (creating translucent glassy glazes) but has virtually been removed from the American ceramic market to prevent its use in pottery making. A particular blend of components will produce a glaze with a specific *melting point*. A melting point is the temperature at which the glaze becomes molten glass. This melting point must match the vitrification temperature of the tile's clay body (low, mid-range, or high fire). Additional components in glazes are colorants and opacifiers. Most people are familiar with the blues produced with cobalt. Chrome, copper, iron, and manganese are also popular glaze colorants, while tin and zirconium are used to make glazes opaque.

Glaze ingredients are mixed with water to become liquid glaze. Most of the ingredients don't actually dissolve, but remain suspended in the water. Liquid glaze can be applied to tile in a number of ways, to produce various effects. Spraying glaze (with a spray gun) over the tile surface creates a uniform application (or an air brush can be used to blend one color into another). Pouring glaze

over the tile surface, or dipping the tile into a glaze bath, are traditional methods of applying glaze. Painting individual colors on areas of a tile is still done with a paintbrush by hand. These glaze techniques produce the soft, varied looks associated with art tile. Ceramic *decals* and *photo transfer* techniques allow the tile artist to replicate an image on many tiles. The commercial tile industry has mechanized the glazing process producing consistent, yet generic finishes.

Another glaze effect is produced by raku firing. This is a firing method in which a tile is removed from the kiln (with iron tongs and protective gloves) when it is at about 1800° F. The tile is then placed into a metal canister containing combustible materials such as sawdust, leaves or newspaper, which ignite upon contact with the hot tile. The canister is sealed, smothering the flames and creating an oxygen-deprived atmosphere (called reduction). This process leaves a unique surface effect on each tile. Raku tile is known for its iridescent metallic finishes and distinctive white crackle glazes.

Françoise Choveau, Rex Studio, *Fight*, carved relief and mosaic mural, 22" x 16". *Photograph by John Hoenstine*

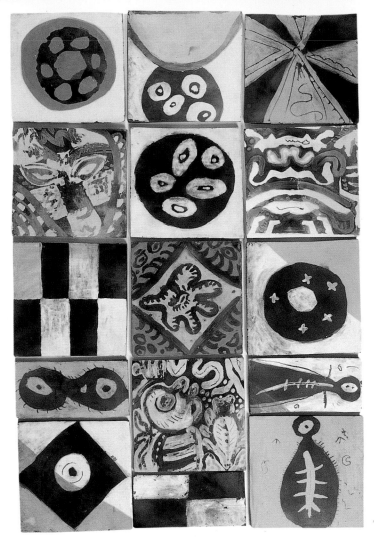

Liz Surbeck Biddle, Handpainted tile,
approximately 4" x 4" each.

Joan Rothchild
Hardin, *Woman
Dressing*,
handpainted tile,
7 3/4" x 11 3/4".
*Photograph by
Steve Glazzo*

Frank Giorgini, Giorgini Studio, *Udu Tile*, 12" x 12" relief tile. *Photograph by Bobby Hansson*

Meet the Artist:
Françoise Choveau, Rex Studio

Françoise was born in Paris, France where she received a degree in philosophy from the Aubert Institute. In 1978 she moved the the United States where she has maintained a studio ever since. In 1990, she started working at the Moravian Tile Works in Doylestown, PA., and it is there that she developed a growing interest in cement and mosaics.

Françoise Choveau, Rex Studio, *Turkey*, sgraffiato tile, 4 1/2" x 4 1/2". *Photograph by John Hoenstine*

Françoise Choveau, Rex Studio, *Elephant*, sgraffiato tile, 11" x 11". *Photograph by John Hoenstine*

34

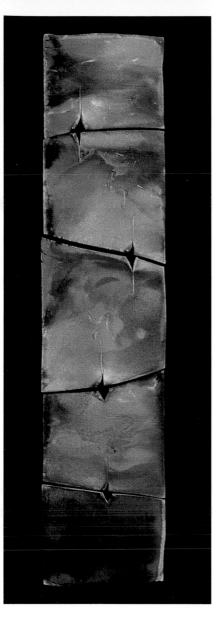

Penny Truitt, raku trapezoid tile
wall piece, 35" x 10".

Véronique Blanchard, Quilt Tile,
mosaic table, 12" x 12" x 18"h.
Photograph by William Collier

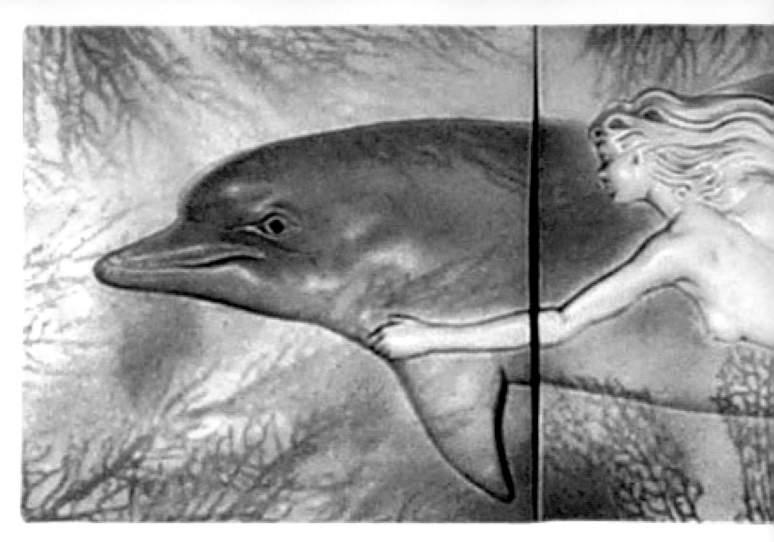

Richard Surving, Surving Studios, *Serena Swimming with a Porpoise* relief mural, each tile 6" x 6".

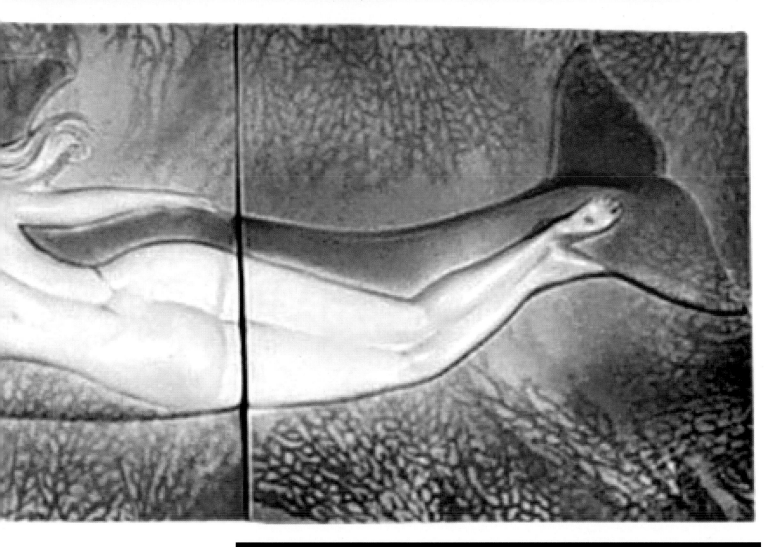

Keith Miller, Sugar Lake Pottery,
Bordered Ferns, leaf impressed tile,
7 1/4" x 4 3/4". *Photograph by Jim
Strickland Photography*

Opposite page: Cristina Acosta,
Cristina Acosta Design,
handpainted *Birds & Flowers* series,
4 1/2" x 4 1/2" each.

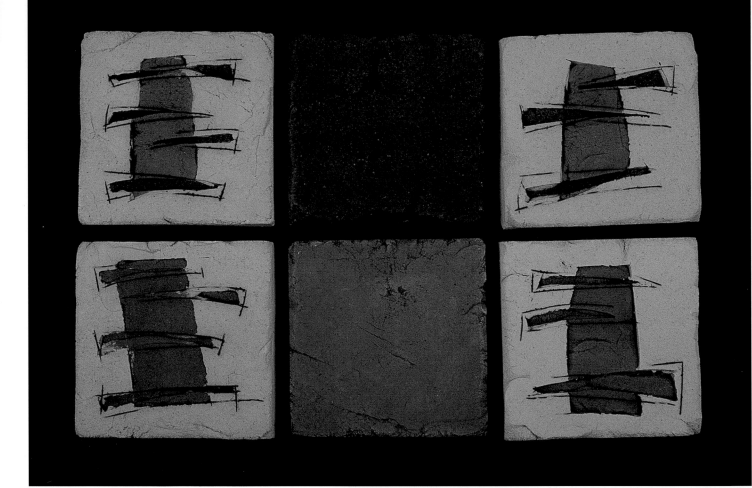

Eui-Kyung Lee has developed a unique encaustic technique to create the patterned designs on these tile, 12" x 8".

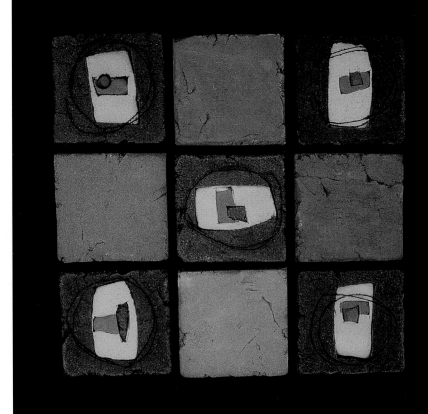

Eui-Kyung Lee, 12" x 12".

Eui-Kyung Lee, 16" x 12"

Eui-Kyung Lee,
12" x 8".

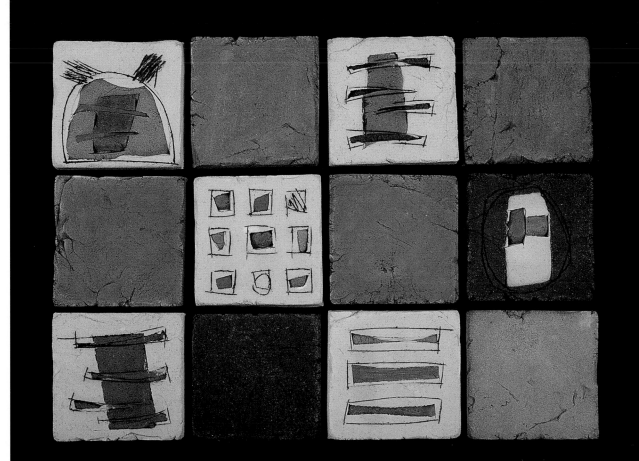

39

Neilsen Amon and Ruby Levesque, Amon Art Tile, *Roundel* relief tile, 4" x 4". *Photograph by Herman Estevez*

Neilsen Amon and Ruby Levesque, Amon Art Tile, *Roundel* relief tile array. *Photograph by Herman Estevez*

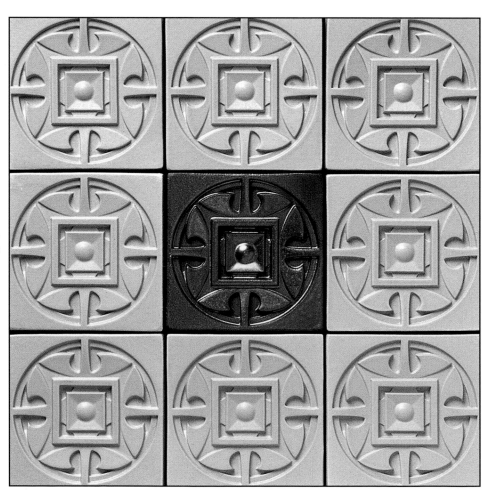

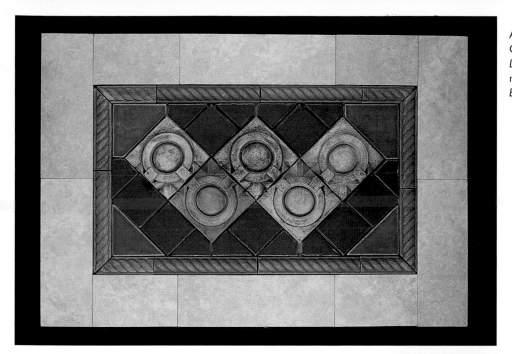

Anne & Edward Nocera, Nocera Art Tile Company, tile panel, 7 3/4" x 4 3/4", *Chain-Link Terra Cotta Block Corner* set with field tile, rope molding and limestone. *Photograph by Edward Nocera*

Lynda Curtis, L. Curtis Designs, *Bestiares et Genies*, sgraffiato tile panel, 10" x 10". *Photograph by Lisa Bogden*

Alison Sawyer, Bayfire Studios, raku relief tile.

41

Meet the Artist:
Frank Bosco

"There's a thread of intent that runs through all my work regardless of its content, and that is to balance aspects of the process that I can control with those that I cannot. Inherent to all ceramic endeavors is the element of chance. I'm always looking for ways to relinquish the control over how a piece is resolved, and to strive for ways which allow the vicissitudes of the process to reach through."

Frank Bosco, Burnt Opera House, modified encaustic technique tile, 60" x 60". *Photograph by Les Helmers*

Steven and Susan Kemenyffy, *Waterlilly II*, 12" x 12" raised line tile. *Photograph by Ed Bernik Photography*

Steven and Susan Kemenyffy, *A Moment in Time*, 28" x 28" raku tile. *Photograph by Ed Bernik Photography*

Celine Quemere, Quemere
International, porcelain relief tile.

Diane Winters, Winters Tileworks,
4-Leaf Wreath, 8" x 8".

44

Chapter Four

How Art Tile is Made

Though techniques can be as varied as designs, this chapter discusses many of the hand processes that go into making art tile.

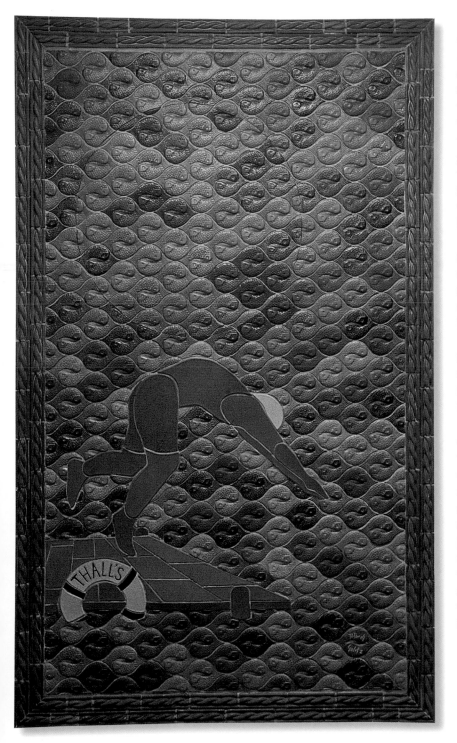

The first step is designing the tile. Tile makers today draw from a myriad of influences and inspirations when designing tile. The basic size and shape of the tile may be determined by industry standards, a customer's request, or dictated by the pattern itself. The tile maker will first render the design on paper (some prefer to draw by hand, while others employ computers and design programs). The drawing must be sized to allow for the shrinkage rate of the clay body (which generally ranges from 5% to 12%). Copy machines which enlarge and reduce by degrees are a great help with this step.

The tile maker must then decide what the surface of the tile will be like. If it is to have a smooth surface, a custom tile cutter may be designed and fabricated to cut individual tile from a rolled sheet of clay. The sheet of clay can also be imprinted with a texture before the cutter is used. If the tile is to be a relief tile, an original model tile must be carved. Many tile makers fashion the model from oil-based (modelling) clay which does not dry, shrink or harden (as fire clay would) during the carving process.

When the model is complete, a frame of wood or clay is built around it, and the interior of the frame is flooded with plaster. The plaster hardens to create a *mother mold*. The model tile is removed from the mother mold when it is hard but still damp. The mold is then allowed to slowly dry and cure...this can take days or even weeks depending upon its size. After it is dry, the mother mold can be used to create tile that will also be framed and flooded with plaster to make *working molds*. A tile maker will often make dozens of working molds for each tile design. Some working molds are fitted with small air tubes (when

DeBorah Goletz, *Postcards from Sheepshead Bay*, Diver mural, Sheepshead Bay subway station, New York, commissioned by the NY Metropolitan Transportation Authority/Arts for Transit. *Photograph by Ken Karp.*

the plaster is wet) to allow compressed air to pass through the mold later on. This helps release the clay tile during production.

Once the working molds are made and allowed to dry, tile production can begin. The actual process of pressing a tile is relatively simple: Plastic clay is placed into the mold and pounded with a mallet or squeezed with a tile press (a device which applies downward pressure to the mold). Squeezing compresses the clay into the recesses of the mold, then excess clay is cut away. The clay tile remains in the mold until the plaster absorbs enough moisture from it to cause the tile to slightly shrink (15 to 30 minutes). At this point, the mold can be turned upside down, allowing the clay tile to gently drop out.

The tile is still soft at this stage and, as mentioned before, great care must be taken not to handle it in a way that would cause it to bend or warp. Tile is dried slowly and evenly until it is bone dry. This can take days or even weeks depending upon the humidity in the studio. A tile maker's schedule may be slowed by several weeks during a rainy season to allow the tile to fully dry before firing. When bone dry, the tile is ready to be fired.

When loading the tile into the kiln for a bisque firing, flat and evenly textured tile may be stacked upon each other or along their edges to rest on the kiln's shelves. Tile is loaded into the kiln by hand, one at a time, and supported so as to prevent warping during the firing. The bisque firing warms slowly, typically taking five to twelve hours to reach a temperature of about 1800° F. The length of the firing is dependent upon the size of the kiln and how many tile it contains. Tile makers use *pyrometric cones* which help them to know when the firing is complete. Pyrometric cones are small sticks of clay which are numbered and designed to melt and bend at specific temperatures (i.e., cone #6 bends at 2174° F. and cone #10 bends at 2300° F.). Many kilns have a device (called a *kiln sitter*) which holds a pyrometric cone and will shut the kiln off when the cone bends at the proper temperature.

When the firing is complete, a kiln must remain closed to allow it to cool for approximately the same amount of time that it took to reach the firing temperature. Once cool, the tile can be unloaded and glazed.

Liquid glaze is applied and quickly dries to a powdery coating which rests on the surface of the tile. Before it is fired, the glaze coating can be scratched and smeared if mishandled. Care must be taken to avoid such damage when loading the tile back into the kiln. Many tile makers wear latex or rubber gloves to protect their hands from the caustic effects of the unfired glaze. Unlike the bisque firing, tile cannot touch each other in the kiln during the glaze firing. This is because the glaze becomes molten glass as it is heated and will fuse to anything it touches. The bottom of the tile is not glazed as this would cause it to fuse to the kiln's shelf.

Some tile makers apply multiple layers of glaze to achieve depth of color. These glazes may be applied all at one time, or the tile may be re-fired as each new layer of glaze is added.

The glaze firing does not warm as slowly as the bisque firing, because the H_2O has already been fired out of the clay body. Glaze firing proceeds at a moderate rate to allow the necessary chemical processes to occur.

After the glaze firing, the kiln is again cooled slowly, this time to avoid causing glaze problems or cracks developing in the tile. The tile are then unloaded from the kiln, packed into boxes and shipped to the installation site.

Art tile must usually be ordered a number of weeks prior to installation. The time it takes to fill an order is based upon the type of tile desired, and the production capacity of the tile studio. The schedule will also take into consideration the drying time of the tile.

A Note to Would-Be Tile Makers

How-to information on tile making is available from books (including Frank Giorgini's *Handmade Tile*), magazines (such as *Ceramics Monthly, Clay Times, Studio Potter*) and workshops with tile makers. The Tile Heritage Foundation and many colleges with ceramics programs offer courses in tile making. The internet has become a valuable resource for technical information about everything from mold making to glaze formulation. Discussion-group sites such as Clayart Network connect thousands of clay artists who respond to queries from beginners and professionals alike. Technologies and resources formerly available only to the commercial industry are now available to individual clay artists and made public through trade magazines such as *Ceramics Industry*.

Meet the Artists:
Karim and Nawal Motawi,
Motawi Tileworks, Inc.

As their brochure explains, Motawi Tile is made by the sibling duo of Karim and Nawal Motawi and their trusty staff. Nawal studied sculpture, ceramics and glaze chemistry at the University of Michigan, and tile making at Pewabic Pottery. Nawal runs the design studio and business office. She designs most of the tile, installations and glazes. Karim, also educated at the U of M, is an adept moldmaker, kiln fireman, glazer and sweet talker. Karim runs the production studio.

Motawi Tileworks, Inc., detail.

Motawi Tileworks, Inc., decorative fireplace relief tile by Nawal Motawi, design by Garnet Johnson, mixed with blue commercial tile

Meet the Artists:
Norma and Kirsten Hanlon, Fresh Fish Ceramic Tiles

Norma Hanlon and Kirsten Hanlon are a mother-daughter team who collaborate to produce Fresh Fish Ceramic Tiles. The first tile they made was sunfish tile created for a family bathroom. These tile were the inspiration for a line of handcrafted ceramic tile incorporating images from the natural world inspired by the lake near the Hanlon home in south Minneapolis and the wilds and woods of the north country.

Norma Hanlon and Kirsten Hanlon, Fresh Fish Ceramic Tiles, concept display board featuring *Fruit & Veggie* series tile, 7" x 13". *Photograph by Peter Lee.*

Paul Zelenka, Unicorn Studio, *Fleur De Lys*, Medieval series, 6" x 6"

48

Meet the Artist:
Mahoko Dahte

"Clay is a gift from Mother Earth. I would like to use this gift to create something that carries a message of peace in our world and also projects something of the Asian culture and philosophy to my adopted country, America. I strongly want to convey messages of peace, tranquility, and harmony with our environment through my art."

Mahoko Dahte,
Sakura, 19" x 9 1/2".
Photograph by Lynn's Lens Photography

Sonoma Tilemakers, *Versailles* and *Empire* tile, 4" x 4" each, are part of Sonoma's *Stellar Design* series. Coordinating sink design, Nancy Epstein.

Neilsen Amon and Ruby
Levesque, Amon Art Tile,
Starburst relief tile, 4" x 4".
Photograph by Herman Estevez

Neilsen Amon and Ruby Levesque, Amon
Art Tile, *Diamonds* relief tile, 4" x 4".
Photograph by Herman Estevez

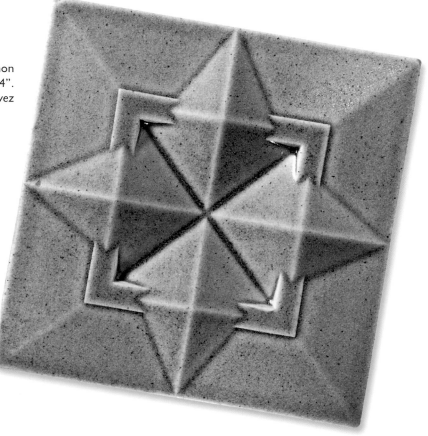

Linda Shields, Atherton Tile Company,
Dynasty insert tile, 1 3/4" x 1 3/4".
Photograph by Don Roper Photography

Joan Rothchild Hardin, *Indian Tree,* handpainted tile, 6" x 12". *Photograph by Erik S. Lieber*

Carolin Meier, California Clay,
Ivy Series Blue molded and
glazed stoneware tile, 4" x 4".

Steven and Susan
Kemenyffy, *Amy IV*, 14" x 14"
raku tile. *Photograph by Ed
Bernik Photography*

Joan Rothchild Hardin, *Victorian Parlor,* handpainted tile, 6" x 12", *Photograph by Steve Glazzo*

Joan Rothchild Hardin, *Reclining Woman,* handpainted tile, 6" x 12". *Photograph by Steve Glazzo*

Sergio Salgado, handpainted relief tile, 12" x 9".

Bev Leviner and Nancy Saragoulis, Hilltop Studio, relief tile, each 5 3/4" x 5 3/4".

Lynda Curtis, L. Curtis Designs, *Medieval Folklore Series,* one of three mosaic panels, 17" x 11". *Photograph by James Shanks*

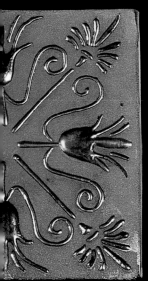

Bev Leviner and Nancy Saragoulis, Hilltop Studio, *Animal Series*, relief tile, largest tile is approximately 5" x 5" each.

Margaret Licha, Margaret Licha Designs, *Critters*, handpainted tile, 4 1/2" x 4 1/2". *Photograph by Shirley Benedick Frost*

Adriana Baler, Adriana Baler Tiles, *Floral*, 3 7/8" square relief tile set with blue field tile.

Meet the Artist: Véronique Blanchard, Quilt Tiles

Véronique Blanchard is a quilt maker who, one day, decided that she wanted to make tile. She attributes this sudden interest to living in close proximity to the Moravian Tile Works. She traded computer skills for the opportunity to apprentice at a local tileworks, "and that was it ... I was hooked." Now, Véronique translates Amish and traditional folk quilt patterns into tile. "Raised line patterning gives a wonderful tactile feel (to the tile) that reminds me of hand quilting. There's a great connection between the lines in the clay and the feeling I have when I'm doing my hand quilting." Véronique also enjoys the relative immediacy of making tile. "It takes forever to get a quilt done—but I can make a mold of a tile pattern, and within a week, I can have 50 different color combinations of that pattern in tile. So I get to play with the colors in a way that I can't do with hand quilting—it's great."

Véronique Blanchard, Quilt Tiles, *Sampler* display board of 2" x 2" raised line tile.
Photograph by William Collier

Chapter Five

Designing With Tile ────────────────────────────

Kitchens and bathrooms have long been the predetermined enclaves of ceramic tile. The following pages feature beautiful and innovative kitchens, interesting and playful bathrooms, and a variety of other venues in which art tile can be used as a functional and decorative element of your home.

According to Christopher Lowell, cable television's popular home decorating guru, there are seven *layers of design* to consider when planning a room. The first layer includes wall coverings and architectural embellishments; the second layer is flooring. Art tile provides unique and individualized solutions for walls, and floors, as well as new and traditional architectural elements. You may not dare use more than a handful of fabrics in a room for fear of them fighting each other, yet it is possible to mix field tile, cornices, borders, liners and accent tile to create a stunning and unified look. The effect can be wild and energized, or controlled and subtle.

One of most important factors to consider when selecting tile is the lifestyle of the person(s) who will be using the room and the function of the room itself. Whether you are working with a designer or architect, or decorating a space yourself, ask: "What are my lifestyle needs? Will I clean the space myself or have help? Will children or pets will be using the space? Do I need a floor tile that hides dirt? Will I wear shoes or go bare foot in the space? Will the room be used by children or elders who have special needs, such as easy-to-reach sinks or non-skid floors? Will I require special areas to place hot pans or roll out dough? Are appliances, canisters, etc. kept on the counters?" Answer these questions honestly—you are changing your decor, not your lifestyle (and you don't want a hand painted-mural hidden by the microwave)! On the other hand, if you like to keep storage canisters out, you might find ceramic pots that compliment your tile (some tile makers are also potters). The answers to these questions will guide you to choose a look that will enhance, not hamper, your lifestyle.

The next thing to consider when selecting tile, is the feeling you want to experience when you use the room. Is the room to be quiet and relaxing, striking and sophisticated, or lively and playful? Because tile remains where you put it for many, many years, home owners often consider the resale value of their choices. Bruce Levitt, President of Tiles—A Refined Selection, Inc., observes that "when the economy expands, people are willing to do esoteric, non-traditional tile installations. And when the economy falls, people are more concerned about real estate values and more conservative with their tile designs." This usually means choosing neutral-colored tile, though style can still be achieved by blending hues and textures.

Now look carefully at your room. Look for opportunities to highlight selected areas with tile. Leanne Croft of Leanne Croft Interiors feels that ceramic tile has replaced a lot of other design surfaces such as wall coverings, floor coverings, wood moldings and even fabrics. One of her favorite places to use tile instead of fabric is on cornice boards over windows. She contrasts soft fabric curtains with the hard surface of tile. She also commissions tile artisans to handpaint fabric or wall covering patterns onto tile for use in a backsplash.

Art tile have long been used as fireplace surrounds. A beautiful fireplace provides a focal point for a room and sets the tone for the surrounding decor. If you are on a budget (and who isn't?), this can be a good investment of your decorating dollars. Bruce Levitt reports that his company does a lot of fireplaces. "They are small areas where you can do something with art tile that's kind of pricey and big in terms of design, but you're not going to spend too much money."

There are endless ways to decorate with art tile. You might place an inspirational mural on the kitchen backsplash where you prepare food. Or you might install ceramic cornice molding as an added architectural element to the room. Or you could surround a vanity with an edge tile to compliment a chair rail molding. For a subtle, textured effect, you could mix different sized (or shaped) tile in a single color. Even a soap dish set into the wall can become an artistic statement if framed in border tile or set into a mosaic mural. A hardwood floor can look stunning set within a ceramic edge tile or mosaic border, particularly if the tile is repeated on the wall as a baseboard, chair rail, or cornice. Shiny, satin and matte tile finishes can be mixed to break up the monotony of a single color palette. The oft underestimated square tile can be installed as squares, or diamonds, or both (above and below a chair rail molding, for instance) to create a spectacular effect.

For the moment, allow yourself to suspend financial concerns. With a bit of creativity, style can be had in every price range. Where to look for ideas? Well, you've probably already seen art tile in magazines. Ceramic art tile is appearing in ads for everything from faucets to electronics, and its look is imitated in vinyl, linoleum and laminate flooring. Chances are there is a tile showroom near you that carries art tile (see Index of Showrooms and Galleries). And enjoy the images in this book. There is tile to satisfy every taste.

Lynda Curtis, L. Curtis Designs, *Malacate Series* backsplash, 3" square relief tile and 1" x 2" border relief tile set into hand cut field tile. *Photograph by James Shanks*

Lynda Curtis, L. Curtis Designs, *Triclinio* foyer/dining table, handpainted tile, 45"w. x 36"h. x 15"d. *Photograph by Ilisa Katz*

Ginger Dunlap-Dietz, kitchen backsplash with hand and footprint impressed tile, 8" x 8" each, set into commercial field tile. *Photograph by William Gandino*

Ginger Dunlap-Dietz, detail of previous image. *Photograph by William Gandino*

Phyllis Pacin, Phyllis Pacin Ceramic Design, raku tile installation in the kitchen of a yacht. *Photograph by Gary Fox*

Cristina Acosta, Cristina Acosta Design, handpainted tile, 4 1/2" x 4 1/2" each.

Véronique Blanchard, Quilt Tile, raised line bearpaw pattern tile set with commercial tile. *Photograph by William Collier*

Holly P. Walker, backsplash with relief tile and hand-cut terra cotta
field tile, 6" x 90". *Photograph by Leon E. Skipwith*

Donna Schuurhuis, *Elephant* mural,
12" x 12" handpainted on
commerical tile.

Michael F. Dupille, Iridized pressed glass relief tile set in ceramic mosaic tile.

Donna Schuurhuis, *Snowy Egrets
and Sandpiper,* mural,
handpainted on commerical tile.

The Meredith
Collection, by
Ironrock Capital,
Dogwood backsplash
tile from the Distinc-
tive Settings series.

The Meredith Collection, by
Ironrock Capital, *Southwest*
backsplash.

Left: The Meredith Collection, by Ironrock Capital, *Wild Rose and Lattice* tile from the Distinctive Settings series, designed by Jance Lentz.

Bottom right: The Meredith Collection, by Ironrock Capital, Celtic Braid series tile.

Bottom left: The Meredith Collection, by Ironrock Capital, mirror and three inserts are *Dogwood and Roycroft* series relief tile based on Arts and Crafts tile.

Paul Lewing, *Pigs*, handpainted mural for stove hood. *Photograph by Turk's Head Productions, Inc.*

Paul Lewing, *Tropical Fish*, handpainted mural. *Photograph by Turk's Head Productions, Inc.*

Craig Crawford, Tempest Tileworks. Stove hood's decorative inset tile uses photo transfer technique. *Photograph by Bob Sasson*

Craig Crawford, Tempest Tileworks, decorative inset bathroom tile using photo transfer technique. *photograph by Bob Sasson*

Shel Neymark, handpainted kitchen backsplash mural. *Photograph by Herb Lotz*

Shel Neymark, *Undersea Bathroom*, whole room environment. *Photograph by Herb Lotz*

Sonoma Tilemakers, *Carousel and Romanov* series tile. *Trapunto* tile has a quilted look.

Tia Grass, *Island Maidens* mosaic mirror frame, 23" x 18".

Linda Boston, detail of custom relief fireplace surround. *Photograph by Richard Hirneisen*

Meet the Artist:
Linda Boston

"Doing an installation is an exciting venture, beginning with a concept, then a design, then months where everything is in tiny little pieces, until finally, it all comes together in one beautiful effort. This piece was commissioned by a photographer. When viewed as a whole, the fireplace surround appears somewhat classical, but many of its elements are very graphic, including the camera aperture serving as the focal point."

Linda Boston, custom relief tile fireplace surround. *Photograph by Richard Hirneisen*

72

Meet the Artist:
Kristina Baum, Shubunkin Pottery

"The inspiration for this piece came from many hours spent contemplating the fishpond in my backyard. The style was influenced by a book of Chinese fabric designs. I love tile for its ability to decorate in a substantial and permanent manner and enjoy the challenge of designing custom tile to fit in a particular setting."

Kristina Baum, Shubunkin Pottery, *Tranquility* fireplace surround, handpainted relief tile.

Motawi Tileworks, Inc., *Ice Ray* pattern floor tile.

Motawi Tileworks, Inc., fireplace with *Leaves & Berries* relief tile.

Motawi Tileworks, Inc., custom fireplace
with sculpted *Datura* motif.

Motawi Tileworks, Inc., detail of
previous image.

Kim Gore, Kim Gore Hand-Sculpted Tile Co., *Bacchus* fireplace surround. *Photograph by Peter Smith*

Kim Gore, Kim Gore Hand-Sculpted Tile Co., *Medallion* fireplace surround, one of two surrounds for a fireplace which opens into two rooms. *Photograph by Peter Smith*

Kim Gore, Kim Gore Hand-Sculpted Tile Co., *Bacchus* fireplace surround, one of two surrounds for a fireplace which opens into two rooms. *Photograph by Peter Smith*

Phil Raskin, North Prairie Tileworks, fireplace surround.

Phil Raskin, North Prairie
Tileworks, fireplace surround
made with relief tile and various
field tile.

Holly P. Walker, stair risers of hand cut terra cotta field tile with single relief tile, 4" x 4" tile. *Photograph by Leon E. Skipwith*

Paul Zelenka, Unicorn Studio, Medieval series and Celtic series tile, stairway riser design by Lisa Keummel.

Paul Zelenka, Unicorn Studio, detail of stairway risers.

Paul Zelenka, Unicorn Studio, countertop design by Lisa Keummel.

Laura Shprentz, Spiral Studios, *Santa Fe Nicho*, hand carved and painted relief mural, 32" x 24" x 4"deep. *Photograph by Kevin Murphy*

Laura Shprentz, Spiral Studios, *Santa Fe Nicho*, detail showing "false mosaic" relief tile (grout fills the carved relief giving it the appearance of several smaller tile). *Photograph by Kevin Murphy*

Shel Neymark, *Window for Room with no Window*, handpainted and relief wall mural. *Photograph by Herb Lotz*

Shel Neymark, *Tropical Mural with Carmen Miranda Border*, handpainted mural with mosaic border, 14' x 9'. *Photograph by Herb Lotz*

Meet the Artist:
Michelle Griffoul,
Michelle Griffoul Studios

Michelle's brochure tells how over thirty years Michelle Griffoul has thrown, pushed, rolled, torn, pit fired, raku fired, high fired, low fired, sun baked, flocked, painted and otherwise stretched the acknowledged limits of clay. The consummate clay artist, Michelle is a classically trained potter with the eye of a painter and the production skills and sensibilities of a manufacturing engineer...With her sense of design and glazing techniques, Michelle continues to surprise clients by breaking through the traditional boundaries of tile.

Michelle Griffoul, Michelle Griffoul Studios, *Baby Leaves Columns* covered with ceramic mosaic tile.

Michelle Griffoul, Michelle Griffoul Studios, *Magnolia Bench,* ceramic mosaic tile, 60" in length.

Michelle Griffoul, Michelle Griffoul Studios, *Fallen Leaves* chaise, ceramic mosaic tile, 60" in length.

Nancy Holcomb, custom
ceramic gates, handpainted
mosaic mounted on steel
structure.

Nancy Holcomb, custom residen-
tial fountain, handpainted mosaic.

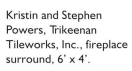

Kristin and Stephen Powers, Trikeenan Tileworks, Inc., fireplace surround, 6' x 4'.

Kristin and Stephen Powers, Trikeenan Tileworks, Inc., custom hearth, 30" x 48".

Kim Adams, Custom-Made Tile, mosaic backsplash.

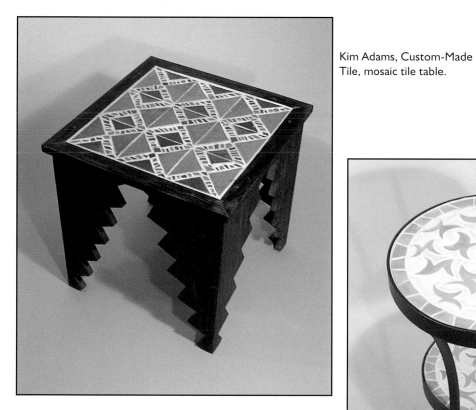

Kim Adams, Custom-Made
Tile, mosaic tile table.

Kim Adams, Custom-Made Tile,
custom mosaic tile table.

Katherine Hackl, *Aesops Fable Table,* 18" x 32" x 18".

Nancy Chevalier-Guido, custom tile table top.

Frank Giorgini, Giorgini Studio, *Afro Lizard Fireplace*, carved relief tile.

Frank Giorgini, Giorgini Studio, relief tile tables, approximately 12" x 12" x 18".

Françoise Choveau, Rex Studio, dog house with ceramic tile "bones". *Photograph by John Hoenstine*

Françoise Choveau, Rex Studio, large planter, 22" x 16" x 12"h. *Photograph by John Hoenstine*

88

Steve de Perrot, Pots by de Perrot, glazed design end table 13 1/2" x 13 1/2" x 18"h.
Photograph by Larry Lefever

Steve de Perrot, Pots by de Perrot, glazed design coffee table, end table, foyer table, foyer table measures 32 1/2" x 13 1/2" x 33"h.
Photograph by Larry Lefever

89

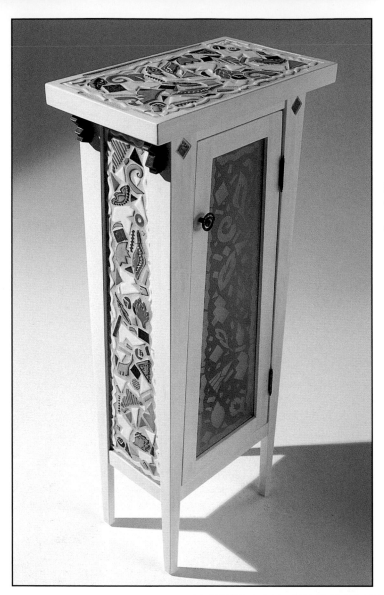

Rosalyn Tyge, Tyge Tile/Art, cabinet with mosaic tile 20"w. x 45"h. x 11"d. *Photograph by John Robert Williams*

Rosalyn Tyge, Tyge Tile/Art, tiled corner table 32"w. x 20"d. x 28"h. *Photograph by John Robert Williams*

Chapter Six

Visiting A Tile Showroom

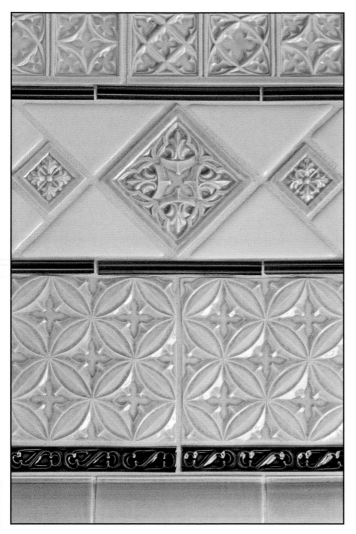

Sonoma Tilemakers, *Stellar* series carved relief tile and skinny liners create a concept board, 18" x 12".

Walking into a tile showroom can be like entering an old world villa or a fantasy play castle. What you are experiencing is tile's ability to transform a space into a timeless, sumptuous, stylish environment. It is easy to become overwhelmed in a large showroom filled with so many lush textures and staggering visual arrays. At first one can't help but feel like a kid in a candy shop as your eyes dart from one display to the next. Unless you are just gathering design ideas, don't try to view the entire showroom yourself. A knowledgeable salesperson can guide you to the type of tile you are interested in, before your eyes glaze with overstimulation.

Like marriage, choosing ceramic tile is a long-term commitment and not one to be entered into lightly. Begin with a tile that *really* appeals to you *and* meets your lifestyle needs. If you find one that you love, but it doesn't suit your lifestyle...keep looking. Once you find the right tile, the one you love, fondle it (smaller displays can be removed from the wall). It's amazing how much information you can gather through tactile contact. Ask the salesperson more about the tile. Is it an accent tile? A field tile? A border tile? What other colors does it come in? Then put the tile down and continue to look around. After a few minutes, return to see if you still love it. Then go home and think about it. If one is available, take a sample home and live with it for a few days (a refundable deposit is usually required to take home a sample piece of art tile). If you still love it after a day or so, chances are you have a good starting point for your design.

You may consider hiring a tile designer to help you achieve the look you wish to create. A tile designer can help select tile borders and trims to work with, and compliment the tile you have selected. A tile designer can also help organize your choices to produce the desired mood of the room.

In some showrooms, the salespersons are trained to help you with the design process as well. At Artistic Tile, members of the design sales team work with customers one-on-one. Sitting with the customer, a birds-eye view sketch is rendered based on the measurements of the room. Doors, windows and fixtures are penciled in. This view allows the customer to see floor tile, baseboard molding, wall tile, wall murals, chair rails, cornices, borders and decorative inserts as they are added to the drawing. These choices are based upon the customer's concept of the room. Sometimes an elevation (front view) of a single wall is also drawn, and colored in, to help the customer visualize the finished project. A fee is charged for this design work, but it is well worth it, since the fee is directly applied to the purchase price of the tile. The customer does not leave with the design drawing (which could be duplicated at another showroom). But usually a sample tile can be purchased (the cost would also be credited to the overall job).

If you are considering using a custom-designed tile, or even a standard design with a custom color, Bruce Levitt advocates ordering a *strike-off* (a made-to-order sample tile). "Before you order a hundred pieces, order a strike-off to see if you like it. It's insurance. If you like it, you put it on the wall, if you don't, you'll be happy you saw it (before placing the large order)."

Discuss your budget with the salesperson. Salespeople know what parts of your selection can be modified to cut the cost but retain the look. Its often possible to substitute a lower-priced field tile, with little variation to the overall design. The salesperson can also help you estimate the labor costs of the installation.

So what can you expect to pay for a bathroom? Artistic Tile came up with these estimates for a typical 5' x 7' bathroom:

Stone and glass installation: $3,000–$5,000
Ceramic tile installation: (mix of commercial and art tile), $1,500–$8,000
Art tile only: Prices could go up to $11,000.

Showroom Vocabulary

This is a short list of terms and definitions used in a tile showroom.

bacello: half round tile molding
bar liner: thin, very flat liner tile
baseboard molding: tile placed along the bottom edge of a wall where it meets the floor
bead liner: liner tile with raised bumps or "beads" on the surface
border tile: used to frame field tile, often used as a chair rail
braid: molding tile which looks like braid
bull nose tile: tile designed to curve over an edge or corner
color way: retail term for color
concept boards: mounted display of complimentary tile, such as liners and moldings
corner tile: tile which curves around an inside or an outside corner
cornice: architectural molding which runs around the top of a room
cove piece: a hollow, quarter-round piece of molding tile
dental molding: a molding design imitating a row of teeth
display boards: mounted display containing a group of a type of tile (such as a group of bar liners)
edge tile: liner or border tile
egg and dart pattern: historical molding pattern which resembles eggs and darts
field tile: tile used as a background for decorative tile
insert: decorative tile set into a group of field tile
molding: architectural trim tile
liner: narrow strip tile used to create stripes, or frame a border tile
mosaic: design created with small cut pieces of tile (or stone, or glass)
mosaic borders: customized or standard, these bands of mosaic tile are pre-mounted on mesh
mural: series of tile which group together to form an image
ogee: half round border tile with attached lip (often used as a decorative edge on a counter top)
plant-ons: small decorative tile motifs designed to be affixed to the surface of installed tile (or over the grout joints)
profile: a style of tile
running pattern: a repeating pattern
strike-off: made-to-order sample tile
tesserae: a small piece of tile used in mosaic work
vignette: showroom installation representing a room, and featuring flooring, wall tile and a lifestyle component (such as furniture or a countertop). Vignettes help customers visualize what the tile will look like installed in a home.

Opposite page: Sonoma Tilemakers, *Sonoma Reserve* tile feature *Camelot* plant-ons in this showroom vignette.

Meet the Artist:
Linda Shields, Atherton Tile Company

"As an artist I am committed to preserving and perpetuating the art of tile making. I gain inspiration from history, which is rich with design. Nature provides me with infinite possibilities in shape, texture, and color. I embellish my tile with glazes that compliment the natural stone they are designed to accompany."

Linda Shields, Atherton Tile Company, *Olivia* insert tile, 1 3/8" x 1 3/8" each, set in a field of stone tile. *Photograph by George O'Hanlon*

Natalie Surving, Surving Studios, concept board
showing a border of 4" tile set with liner tile,
bacello, and 2" bug insert tile in field tile. *Photograph
by Richard Surving*

Natalie Surving, Surving Studios,
array of 1" x 1" tile. *Photograph by
Richard Surving*

Natalie Surving, Surving Studios, *Vine Scotia* trim tile. *Photograph by Richard Surving*

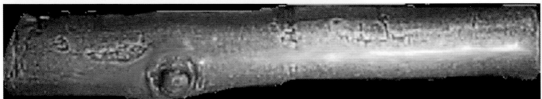

Natalie Surving, Surving Studios, *Branch* trim tile. *Photograph by Richard Surving*

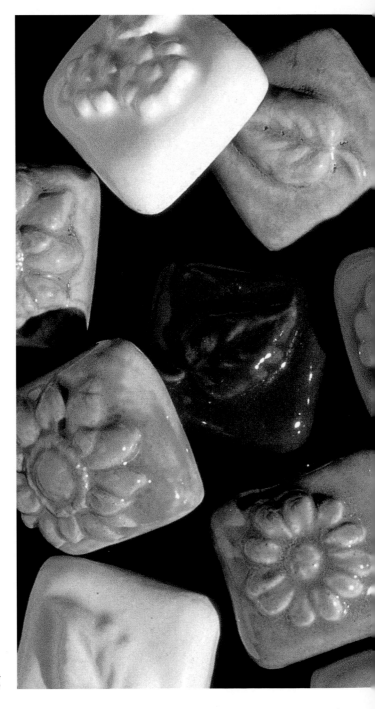

Kim Gore, Kim Gore Hand-Sculpted Tile Co., handpainted relief border tile, 2" x 6". *Photograph by Peter Smith*

Kim Gore, Kim Gore Hand-Sculpted Tile Co., drawer pulls, approximately 1 1/2" x 1 1/2" each. *Photograph by Peter Smith*

Meet The Artist:
Cristina Acosta, Cristina Acosta Design

After graduating from the University of Oregon in 1988, with a degree in Painting, Cristina worked in the outdoor advertising industry for two years, painting murals and lettering. In 1991, she taught art classes while developing her studio business which has propelled her art images from the walls of her Oregon studio to the walls of homes nationwide. "My goal is to bring color, style and a sense of whimsy into every image I create."

Cristina Acosta, Cristina Acosta Design, handpainted *Rainforest* series, 4 1/2" x 4 1/2" each.

Margaret Licha, Margaret Licha Designs, *City Dogs-Country Dogs*, handpainted tile, 4 1/2" x 4 1/2" each. *Photograph by Shirley Benedick Frost*

Kristin and Stephen Powers, Trikeenan Tileworks, Inc., *Shell Mozaik Table*, 17" x 21".

Meet the Artists:
Ann & Edward Nocera, Nocera Tile Co.

Ann and Edward Nocera were originally potters, struggling with their business. On a trip to the Smithsonian museum Anne fell in love with the tile floor in the Arts and Industry building. She suddenly said "You know what? People need tile. They don't need pots. Let's make tile." And that's really how they came to make tile. That was seventeen years ago. Anne reports it took about seven years to get going, but for the last 10 years, they have been selling through showrooms, designers, builders, and the internet.

Anne & Edward Nocera, Nocera Art Tile Company, architectural relief panel, 19 1/2" x 19 1/2", consisting of rectangular border tile, oval accessory piece, and a corner piece framing square field tile.
Photograph by Edward Nocera

Norma Hanlon and Kirsten Hanlon, Fresh Fish Ceramic Tiles, concept display board featuring *Coffee & Tea* series tile, 7" x 10". *Photograph by Peter Lee*

Rosalyn Tyge, Tyge Tile/Art, four tile (square tile measures 6" x 6" each). *Photograph by Don Rutt*

Craig Crawford, Tempest Tileworks, display board showing relief tile and border set with field tile. *Photograph by Bob Sasson*

Chapter Seven

Tile Trends ——————————————————————————————

Arnon Zadok, master tilesetter and owner of Ceramica Arnon showroom, sheds light on recent tile trends:

"Ceramic tile has a long history. Styles do not change from year to year like the fashion industry, but rather evolve slowly, over decades. When the American stock market dropped in the 1980s, people chose to restore, rather than remodel their kitchens and bathrooms. This caused people look with more interest at things that were antique and worn out. The worn, antique aesthetic became big. At that time, homes were being decorated in Post Modern, Santa Fe, and Art Deco styles. These three styes all used similar colors: pastel blues, pinks and lots of gray. In the 1990s that trend died; nobody wanted to look at gray tile anymore. Art tile became more popular, and people began to install them with stone and other materials."

Current trends include handpainted tile, in both traditional and contemporary patterns, which continues to maintain its appeal. Unglazed stoneware tile is making an appearance as a popular alternative to stone. Glass and metal tile is being mixed with ceramic tile and stone. Plant-ons are being mounted on field tile to add texture and character. Inserts are getting smaller, border tile is getting bigger, and texture is everywhere you look. Although glazes and color choices are more diverse than ever, Americans are interested in the timelessness of off-whites, creams and biscuit colors to create rich, luxurious looks.

Stone is a popular alternative to ceramic tile. The color of stone, however, varies greatly from piece to piece, and this unpredictability might make ceramic tile a more reliable alternative. Stone also needs to be sealed. Arnon Zadok suggests the following to his customers: "If you don't have a maid, and you are not willing to get on your hands and knees to take care of stone, you probably should opt for ceramic tile, which requires less maintenance." Commercial tile can imitates the look of stone while providing the easy care of a ceramic surface. Stone-look ceramic borders and accent pieces are also being produced as an economical alternative to carved stone.

———————————————————————————

Antiquities Tile, Weisman, Spaulding Design, Inc., unglazed, woodfired stoneware tile set with stone field tile in this showroom vignette.

Susan Dunis, Dunis Studios, *Modern Surfaces Collection*, assorted relief tile.

Mark Oliver, Metal relief tile
with Celtic knot.

Michael F. Dupille, *Killer Whale*, 8" x 16", fused glass tile.

Linda Shields, Atherton Tile Company, *Diamond* insert tile, 1 3/8" x 1 3/8" each, set in a field of stone tile. *Photograph by George O'Hanlon*

Geometry as an Influence

It's hard not to be mesmerized by the geometry of even a simple square tile, repeated endlessly, over an expanse of wall. The nature of tile implies repetition...repetition which involves geometry. The geometry is created by the grout joints of the tile which generally draw a viewer's eye.

Tile artisans use geometry to create this magic. For example, I wanted to create an undulating grout line to emulate water for my fish tile. Geometry can also be used to fool the eye: the photos in this section all use a single tile shape to create a complex pattern (look carefully—some appear to use more than one tile shape, but it's an illusion).

Pat Wehrman, Dodge Lane Potters Group, *Wilma's Cafe* tile, commissioned installation.

Neilsen Amon and Ruby Levesque, Amon
Art Tile, *Ball & Cross* relief tile, 4" x 4".
Photograph by Herman Estevez

Neilsen Amon and Ruby Levesque, Amon Art
Tile, *Ball & Cross* relief tile array, 4" x 4" each.
Photograph by Herman Estevez

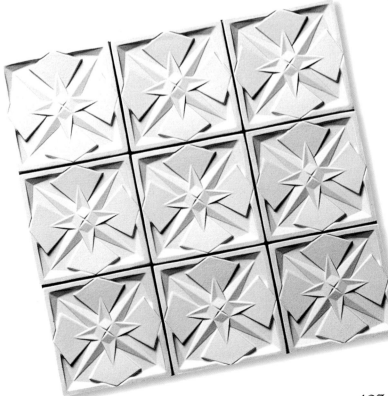

Neilsen Amon and Ruby Levesque, Amon Art
Tile, *Starburst* relief tile array, 4" x 4" each.
Photograph by Herman Estevez

Laura Lyn Stern, Sculptural Designs, *Leaf and Star* relief tile, 4" x 4".

Laura Lyn Stern, Sculptural Designs, *X and O* relief tile, 4" x 4".

Carolin Meier, California Clay,
Acanthus, 4" x 4" terra cotta
encaustic tile.

Phyllis Pacin, Phyllis Pacin Ceramic
Design, *Urban Amoeba. Photograph by
Gary Fox*

Classical Influences

Tile artists often draw from the past for inspirational designs and patterns. The look is ageless and the appeal is endless. Architectural elements from every era are incorporated into everything from cornices to floor tile. Mythical images and medieval artifacts lend themselves to the molded designs of pressed tile. Ancient Celtic patterns, 15th century paintings, petroglyphs and early prints all find themselves fodder for the tile artists of today.

Pedro Leitao, Solar Tiles, handpainted reproduction of an 18th century Portuguese mural on handmade tile, approximately 20" x 15".

Pedro Leitao, Solar Tiles, handpainted reproduction of an 18th century Dutch mural on handmade tile, approximately 25" x 30".

Paul Zelenka, Unicorn Studio, *Rotondelle*, Medieval series, 6" x 6".

Meet the Artist: Paul Zelenka, Unicorn Studio

Paul Zelenka came to the United States in 1983 as a political refugee from Czechoslovakia. He landed in Salt Lake City where he worked for CNC, but was seeking a more satisfying career. In 1995 he read Frank Giorgini's *Handmade Tile* and became "obsessed" about making tile. Tile making satisfied his soul, though not his bank account. Like many artists who turn to a new medium, Paul had a host of technical problems which he had to resolve. "There were so many frustrations ... cracked and ugly pieces ... and lots of cussing and swearing." But within two years, Paul's tile making became a full-time business. Now his tile is represented in showrooms from coast to coast. Paul also does custom tile work and restorations in the Salt lake City area.

Paul Zelenka, Unicorn Studio, *Branche*, Medieval series, 6" x 6"

111

Tania Huusko and Diana Kirk Patrick for Brittany & Coggs, fireplace relief tile was inspired by classic European & American Arts and Crafts designs.

Kim Gore, Kim Gore Hand-Sculpted Tile Co., *Bacchus,* carved relief tile, 8" x 8".
Photograph by Peter Smith

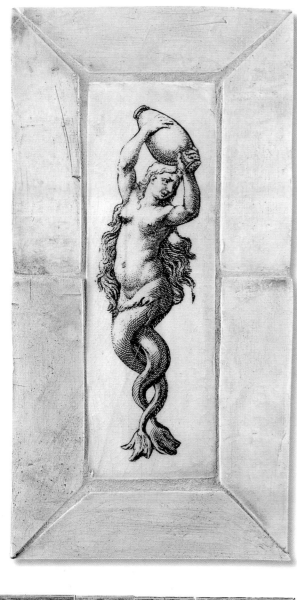

Craig Crawford, Tempest Tileworks, *Poseidon's Nymph,* photo transfer technique. *Photograph by John Corbet*

Craig Crawford, Tempest Tileworks, *Dolphin with Greek Key Border,* handpainted tile with relief border. *Photograph by John Corbet*

Craig Crawford, Tempest Tileworks, *Punchinello,* photo transfer technique, 6 3/4" x 9 1/2". *Photograph by Bob Sasson*

113

Kristin and Stephen Powers, Trikeenan
Tileworks, Inc., *Spring Dance*, handpainted
and relief mural, 4' x 2'.

Opposite page
Top: Bonnie Smith, handpainted cobalt blue-on-white
glazed tile, approximately 4" x 4" each.

Bottom: Bonnie Smith, handpainted cobalt blue-on-white
glazed tile, approximately 4" x 4" each.

Nature as an Influence

It's not surprising that tile, formed from earth (clay),
water, and fire is often used to illustrate images from nature. These tile pay homage to their humble beginnings,
and celebrate the world in which they exist.

Kristin and Stephen Powers, Trikeenan
Tileworks, Inc., *Forest Creature* series,
3" x 6" and 2" x 2" tile.

Alison Sawyer, Bayfire Studios,
raku relief tile.

Alison Sawyer, Bayfire Studios,
raku relief tile.

Meet the Artist:
Keith Miller, Sugar Lake Pottery

Keith's interest in pottery began with an art class in junior high school and early visits to Seagrove, North Carolina. As with many young people, though, he was discouraged from pursuing art in favor of a more "academic" curriculum. After studying history at the University of North Carolina at Chapel Hill, Keith paid the bills as a hair designer and sometimes actor and model. At the age of forty, he decided it was time to return to his true passion, so he established Sugar Lake Pottery. Today, he donates materials and time to encourage local middle school students to pursue their own interests in pottery.

Keith Miller, Sugar Lake Pottery, leaf impressed botanical tile, 4" x 4" each. *Photograph by Jim Strickland Photography*

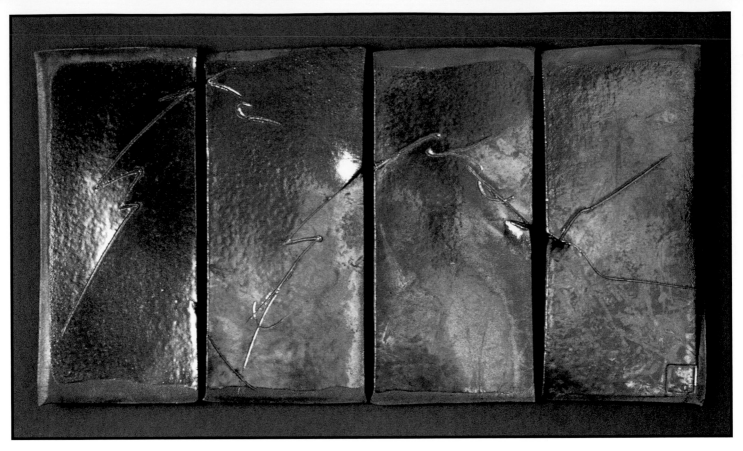

Penny Truitt, *Sundown Sea II*, raku mural, 11 3/4" x 19".

Meet the Artist:
Sally Mason, Black Dog Clayworks

"The rocks and spires of the Chiricahua Mountains grabbed a piece of my soul and transposed themselves into the clay. Soon to join them were the cliff dwellings of the ancient citizens of the Southwest. To be a vehicle of the quiet, timeless passion of those huge pieces of nature is a blessing, and to spend hours lost in the angles and shadows of rocks brings me great joy and peace."

Sally Mason, Black Dog Clayworks,
Land of the Grandparents carved relief
tile, 10 1/2" x 9 1/2".

Laura Shprentz, Spiral Studios, detail, *Walled Garden*, handpainted
relief tile, tree tile is 8" x 8", other tile are 4" x 6 1/2" and 4" x 2 1/2".

Laura Shprentz, Spiral Studios,
Tapestry Tile group, carved
relief tile, 8" x 8" each.
Photograph by D. James Dee

Donna Schuurhuis, *Tree* mural,
12" x 12", handpainted on
commerical tile.

Donna Schuurhuis, *Angelfish* tile,
6" x 6" handpainted design on
commericial tile.

Stephen F. Fabrico.
Photograph by Bob Barrett

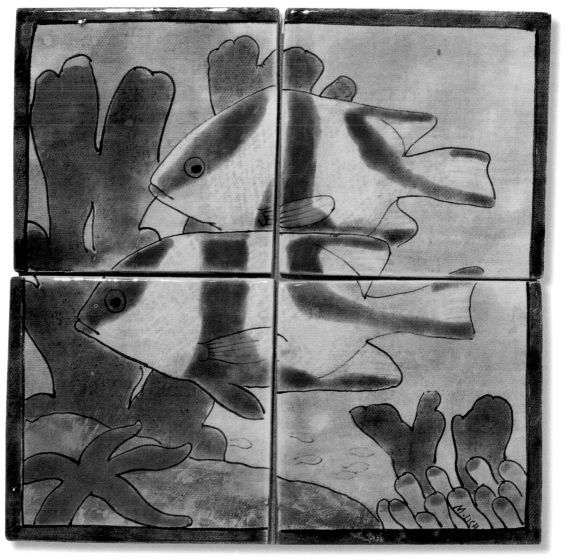

Margaret Licha, Margaret Licha
Designs, *Fish Mural*, handpainted
tile, 4 1/2" x 4 1/2". *Photograph
by Shirley Benedick Frost*

121

Frank Giorgini, Giorgini Studio, *Toucan*, carved relief tile, 6" x 6". *Photograph by Bobby Hansson*

Frank Giorgini, Giorgini Studio, *Elephant*, carved relief tile, 6" x 6". *Photograph by Bobby Hansson*

Meet the Artist:
Natalie Surving, Surving Studios

20 years ago, ceramist Natalie Surving and her artist husband Richard bought a dilapidated old Gristmill in Middleton, New York. Their intention was to rebuild it as a home and studio. After seven years of rebuilding, when it was almost complete, it burned to the ground. With no studio, and facing the prospect of stoking a wood stove all winter until they could rebuild in the spring, an ad for sunny Mexico caught their eye. They arrived in Mexico on Christmas eve with no contacts and little money, but fate brought them together with Felipe Vasquez in Delores Hidalgo. Felipe didn't speak English, so they showed him a photograph of their burned home, and he sent them to his son's tile factory. There they were given clay and a place to work, in exchange for only their friendship...a friendship which has now lasted 13 years. They have since rebuilt their New York home and studio, but return to Mexico each winter.

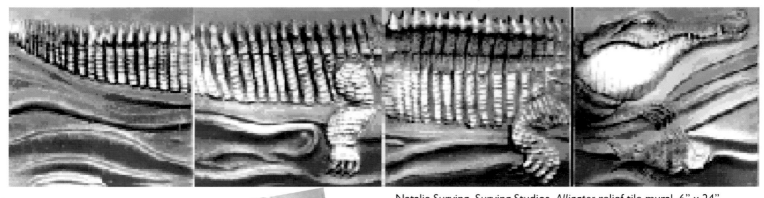

Natalie Surving, Surving Studios, *Alligator* relief tile mural, 6" x 24", Water World Collection. *Photograph by Richard Surving*

Natalie Surving, Surving Studios, *Octopus* relief tile, 6" x 6", Water World Collection. *Photograph by Richard Surving*

Natalie Surving, Surving Studios, *Lion Fish* relief tile, 6" x 6", Water World Collection. *Photograph by Richard Surving*

Rosalyn Tyge, Tyge Tile/Art,
hexagon sun tile, approximately
12" wide. *Photograph by Don Rutt*

Linda Shields, Atherton Tile Company,
Hummingbird insert tile, 1 3/4" x 1 3/4".
Photograph by Don Roper Photography

Pedro Leitao, Solar Tiles, handpainted reproduction of
15th century Italian tile, approximately 5" x 5" each.

Chapter Eight

What to Expect During Installation

For all you do-it-yourselfers out there, consider sitting this one out. Art tile is so variable...tile which is supposed to be the same size isn't; some warps concave, some convex. They are not all the same thickness, or hardness, and there are absolutely *no* straight lines. These are challenges for even the most experienced of tile setters, and could lead the amateur to disaster.

Inexpensive tile can become a work of art in the hands of a creative, deft installer. But a poor installation can ruin the look of even the most expensive tile. If you need to save money, it's better to spend less on the tile than to skimp on the installation costs. Horror stories abound of tile that cracks or falls off the walls after being poorly installed. Leanne Croft tells of a client who purchased large, expensive tile, intending it to be cut and installed in various geometric patterns around an expansive fireplace. Working unattended, an unimaginative installer set the tile in a plain square grid. Obviously, this illustrates the importance of communication with your installer, but even a clear verbal description cannot replace a drawing for conveying your intentions. If possible, try to be present during the installation. Numerous decisions must be made on the spot—ranging from positioning the insets, to deciding which corner of the backsplash should hide the inevitable half tile (you may already be planning to keep an appliance in that corner). Your ideas about tile placement may be very different from your installer's. Talking it over, and laying the tile out together, is the only way to insure the look you want.

Arnon Zadok is a third-generation tile installer who learned the trade from his father at age twelve. He keeps informed of new products and techniques available in his field. Because he also owns his own tile showroom, he understands the special installation needs of ceramic art tile, as well as stone and marble. He advises his clients that some tile needs to be sealed...he explains that many art floor tile are irregular, not flat like commercial tile, and require a mud job setting. And he discusses the fact that heavier tile requires a thicker bed of adhesive for the tile to set in, and that art tile requires a wider grout line to allow for irregularities in the edges.

A common misconception is that a narrow grout joint is easier to keep clean. But Nancy Epstein is quick to discourage customers from a narrow joint. "Having lived with both, I will never go back to a narrow joint again—the wider it is, the easier it is to clean! Goodbye toothbrush! Today the sealers for grout are just so effective, that tile with wider grout joints can really go everywhere."

Elizabeth Grajales, exterior relief tile set into brick, Public School 14, Corona Queens, New York.

And tile can be installed everywhere too. Tile can be installed onto wood, cement (including cement block), drywall, or cement board (used in place of drywall in areas such as kitchens and bathrooms where water damage is a concern). Each of these surfaces requires a different adhesive to set the tile.

If you are planning an installation, keep in mind that tile should never be applied directly to a painted surface without first sealing it with a product such as Bin's Stain Killer. And remember that all surfaces need to be clean and dust free before installation.

Installation Vocabulary

This is a short list of terms and definitions used by installers.

Mud Job: If a floor is not level or stable, a layer of cement (called "mud") is poured over the floor (creating a new surface). These days, thinset cement is used to install tile onto the new surface once it has hardened. (Traditionally, tile installers used to set the tile directly into the wet cement mud). If a mud job is not done properly, there is a risk of cracks developing in the floor.

Bonding agents are designed to enhance the elasticity and adhesion of thinset cement. A bonding agent must be applied to cement board, and to older concrete floors before installing tile. It is not necessary to use a bonding agent when using thin set cement on a new concrete surface or on cement block.

Mastic is used to install tile onto drywall. Mastic is a thinset product which can also be used to install tile over existing tile (this type of installation is not recommended for art tile).

Thinset cement is used to install tile on concrete (including mud jobs) or cement block surfaces. Thinset comes in gray and white colors. If you plan to use white grout, use white thinset to avoid discolorations showing up in the grout.

Multi-purpose glues are available for installing tile on drywall, plaster walls, cement board or plywood.

Grout is a cement material used to fill the joints between tile. It is mixed with water to the consistency of whipped cream and worked into the joints with a stiff, rubber coated tool called a *float*. Sanded grout is mixed with sand and is generally used for floors or wide grout joints. Unsanded grout is generally used for wall tile, tile with soft surfaces, and marble. Bonding agents can be added to grout to enhance adhesion when re-grouting existing tile.

Additives are latex products mixed right in with the thinset or grout when greater elasticity of the setting medium is desired. Additives are recommended for the grout in countertops, to make it less permeable to stains (along with a sealant).

Sealants are applied to grout joints in counters and surfaces where tile is exposed to water. Sealants are also used on some tile finishes (such as crackle or raku glazes) to prevent water and dirt penetration. Sealants should be re-applied approximately every two years.

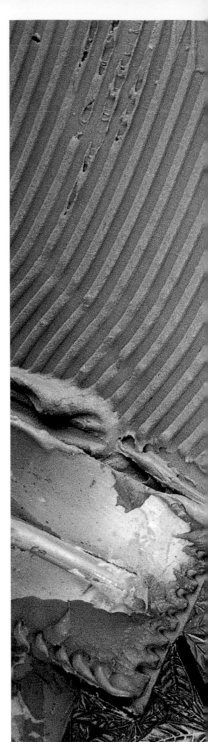

The Care of Tile

Most ceramic tile needs no special maintenance except perhaps a grout sealer. Abrasive cleaners should never be used on ceramic tile. I have installed outdoor projects where the only maintenance required is an occasional cleaning with a hose. Recently I encountered an interesting problem with one of my outdoor murals. Eight months after installation, a white chalky deposit formed on the surface of the tile, particularly around the grout joints. It was most noticeable after a rainstorm. Since the mural was made from a frost-proof clay body engineered for such weather conditions, I looked elsewhere for the cause of the problem. After some investigation, it was determined that the problem was a chemical reaction between the thinset cement and the concrete wall on which the mural was mounted. The problem is called *efflorescence,* which sometimes happens when tile is set onto existing cement walls or floors. Fortunately there was a solution: the mural was washed with a mild sulfamic acid solution to neutralize the reaction.

DeBorah Goletz, Installation of *Historic Artwall*, tile are approximately
6" x 6 1/2" each, John McIntire Library, Zanesville, Ohio.

Michelle Griffoul, Michelle Griffoul Studios, *Fallen Leaves* mosaic insert in sidewalk, 14" x 14".

Linda Shields, Atherton Tile Company, *Classic Kitchen* insert tile, 1 3/4" x 1 3/4", set with ceramic field tile. *Photograph by Don Roper Photography*

Chris Troy, kitchen counter tile, 4" x 4" each.

Chris Troy, backsplash tile, 4" x 4" each.

Meet the Artist:
Nazaré Feliciano

"These images are a construct of two relief tiles. The grout is sand and epoxy. The tile was set to represent a conceptual image of a city, however, I also visualize it as an architectural installation on a large wall or fireplace."

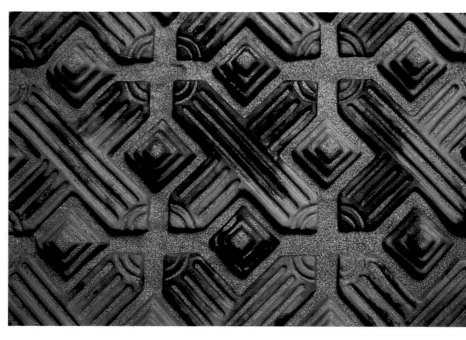

Nazaré Feliciano, *Desert City*.
Photograph by Jean Mazourek

Rosalyn Tyge, Tyge Tile/Art, mosaic wall piece
17" x 25". *Photograph by John Robert Williams*

Pat Wehrman, Dodge Lane Potters Group,
backsplash. *Photograph by Ted White*

Meet the Artist:
Paul Lewing

Paul Lewing always knew he wanted to be an artist. He started painting in oils at the age of eight, and continued it at the University of Montana in Missoula. There he discovered clay and studied with ceramacist Rudy Autio, earning both Bachelor's and Master's degrees in fine arts. After school he began to make pottery, then turned exclusively to tile making in 1986. A former mule packer, horse wrangler, and hunting and fishing guide, Paul often shows his love of mountains and the outdoors in his murals.

Paul Lewing, *Rain Forest* hand painted mural. *Photograph by Turk's Head Productions, Inc.*

Nancy Chevalier-Guido, custom floor tile with mural inset.

Nancy Chevalier-Guido, mosaic, relief tile, and field tile backsplash.

Chapter Nine

Public Art

In a home, art tile expresses the personal tastes and interests of the homeowner. Though enjoyed by visitors, it is intended to be experienced and admired primarily by those who live with it. In contrast, public art is a communal experience intending to educate, or comfort, or stimulate many viewers. It may envelop and transform its environment or be tucked into a niche and discovered in passing. Public art may be bold and revealing or mysterious and alluring. But whatever its approach, it intends to transform the space it occupies, and thereby affect the people that pass through it.

Ceramic material is well suited for the demands of public artwork. Durability is the most important factor for artwork in a public setting. First, it must withstand harsh sun and weather conditions (freezing rain/wind/hail). In the New York subways, as in many public transportation settings, artwork must also endure acid washes to clear away graffiti, steel dust (created by train wheels rolling over the track) and wear and tear from thousands of pedestrians who touch and brush against it.

Sandra Bloodworth, Director of Arts for Transit, for New York's Metropolitan Transportation Authority, explains how ceramic art is used in the subways to uplift the commuting experience. "Many years ago, the New York subway stations had fallen into terrible disrepair, leaving people feeling trapped—affecting their self esteem because they could not afford to take other means of transportation. Today, the stations are all greatly improved, and many boast new artwork of the same quality found in New York museums, including artworks by Elizabeth Murray and Roy Lichtenstein, among others. It's a very public museum all for the price of a fare...and this sends a message to our customers that we really do care about them, and that this is a great place to be."

Artists who are experienced in the public realm can help a company or institution develop a public artwork that can bring it renewed attention, create a focal point, or relieve the boredom of a waiting area. Some artwork involves members of the community in the planning, or even the actual making process. Placed on a facade, a ceramic mural has the power to become a trademark to the public.

Angelica Pozo, detail of *L.A.W.* *Photograph by Hanson Photographic*

Angelica Pozo, *L.A.W.*, silk screened decals on commercial tile. *Photograph by Hanson Photographic*

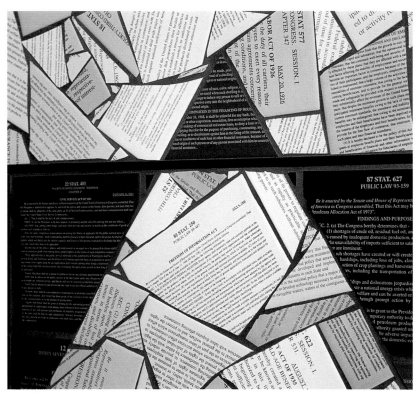

Angelica Pozo, detail of *L.A.W.* *Photograph by Hanson Photographic*

Meet the Artist:
Lynda Curtis, L. Curtis Designs

"From an early age, the art of the storyteller has always fascinated me, sparking an interest in cultures different from my own. As a teenager, I started travelling in the U.S. and abroad. Since this time, my artwork has been a narrative response to the exploration of these various cultures. As the history of each was first recorded pictorially on cave walls, engraved into stone, and in so many instances as an integral part of an architectural structure, ceramic tile seems the perfect medium through which I can translate these stories."

Lynda Curtis, L. Curtis Designs, *Tidal Variations* mural, 3' x 21', Stingray Restaurant, New York, New York. *Photograph by James Shanks*

Meet the Artist:
Ginger Dunlap-Dietz,
Eureka Studios

After making pottery for 25 years, a trip to Thailand and a large tile commission caused Ginger to change focus and start making tile almost exclusively. When Eureka's owners hatched the idea of a show with recycled materials, they suggested she put up a wall using shards, broken pieces, etc. Much of the installation was spontaneous. "It was exciting to see the wall take shape and change as each new group of clay bits went up."

Ginger Dunlap-Dietz, *Eureka Mosaic* entryway, 10' x 7'. *Photograph by William Gandino*

Ginger Dunlap-Dietz, detail of *Eureka Mosaic* entryway. *Photograph by William Gandino*

135

Jean Britt Daves, *Street Dance*, relief mural, 18" x 24".
Photograph by David H. Doggett Bordeaux

Jean Britt Daves, *Waiting at Five Points Station*, hand painted mural, part of a triptych depicting scenes from downtown Atlanta, 18" x 24".

Liz Surbeck Biddle, *Water Rites*, handpainted tile murals for Croton Harmon Rail Road Station, New York, New York Metropolitan Transportation Authority/Arts for Transit.

Liz Surbeck Biddle, *Water Rites*, handpainted tile murals for Croton Harmon Rail Road Station, New York, New York Metropolitan Transportation Authority/Arts for Transit.

DeBorah Goletz, *Postcards from Sheepshead Bay*, facade mural, 8' x 15', Sheepshead Bay subway station, New York, commissioned by the New York Metropolitan Transportation Authority/Arts for Transit. *Photograph by Ken Karp*

DeBorah Goletz, *Postcards from Sheepshead Bay*, facade mural detail, Sheepshead Bay subway station, New York, commissioned by the New York Metropolitan Transportation Authority/Arts for Transit. *Photograph by MTA/Arts for Transit staff photography*

DeBorah Goletz, *Postcards from Sheepshead Bay*, *Fisherman* mural, 7' x 4', Sheepshead Bay subway station, New York, commissioned by the New York Metropolitan Transportation Authority/Arts for Transit. *Photograph by Ken Karp.*

DeBorah Goletz, *Postcards from Sheepshead Bay*, *Boardwalk* mural, 5' x 8', Sheepshead Bay subway station, New York, commissioned by the New York Metropolitan Transportation Authority/Arts for Transit. *Photograph by Ken Karp*

DeBorah Goletz, mural made in collaboration with nursery school children, 3' x 4', Buckle My Shoe Nursery School, New York City.

DeBorah Goletz, *Historic Artwall*, John McIntire Library, Zanesville, Ohio. The 80' x 4', mural features relief panels depicting the history of Zanesville.

DeBorah Goletz, *Historic Artwall*, John McIntire Library, Zanesville, Ohio. Visitors make rubbings of the ceramic relief panels. *Photograph by Eric Goletz*

Steve de Perrot, Pots by de Perrot, mural with names of donors, glazed and relief tile, Lititz public library, Lititz, Pennsylvania. *Photograph by Larry Lefever*

Steve de Perrot, Pots by de Perrot, detail of mural with names of donors, glazed and relief tile, Lititz public library, Lititz, Pennsylvania. *Photograph by Larry Lefever*

Meet the Artist:
Debra Felix, Art Pottery & Tile

"For the past 12 years, I've contracted myself out to different schools and worked with kids to make murals. Teaching them how to work with clay always becomes a learning experience for me, too. First I help them each make practice tile with textures and press molds just to get familiar with the clay. Then we brainstorm and look at visuals, come up with a concept, and develop drawings to transfer onto clay. We use a lot of textures, objects from nature, and press molds. The kids just jump right in and we work together. I figure out how the mural will fit together, but the finished piece is always a wonderful collaborative effort."

Debra Felix *Nature and Design* murals, collaboration with middle-school children, Benchmark School, Media, Pennsylvania. *Photograph by Linda Vanocker*

Debra Felix, *Nature and Design* murals, Benchmark School, Media, Pennsylvania. *Photograph by Linda Vanocker*

Steven and Susan Kemenyffy, detail, *Raku mural for East High School*, Erie, Pennsylvania. *Photograph by Ed Bernik Photography*

Steven and Susan Kemenyffy, *Raku mural for East High School*, Erie, Pennsylvania. *Photograph by Ed Bernik Photography*

Frank Giorgini, Giorgini Studio, waiting room mural,
approximately 3' x 9'. *Photograph by Bobby Hansson*

Nancy Holcomb, handpainted
mosaic mural at Florida's Key West
Airport, 5' x 7'.

Katherine Hackl, *Just So Stories* mural, 8" x 24", one from a series
commissioned by the NJ State House Annex, Trenton, New Jersey.

Katherine Hackl,
*River View and
Woods*, one of a
series of mosaic
murals commis-
sioned by New
Jersey Transit, with
assistance from the
New Jersey State
Council on the Arts.
Funding made
possible by the New
Jersey State
Transportation
Fund.

Elizabeth Grajales, hallway murals, Public School 14, Corona Queens, New York.

Elizabeth Grajales, hallway mural, 24" x 32", Public School 14, Corona Queens, New York.

Elizabeth Grajales, hallway mural, 8" x 16", Public School 14, Corona Queens, New York.

Elizabeth Grajales, design and tile fabrication, Pete Colombo, mosaic fabrication. Mosaic mural surrounded by ceramic relief tile, commissioned by the New York Metropolitan Transportation Authority/Arts for Transit for Pennsylvania Station, New York City.

Elizabeth Grajales, 18" x 18" detail of previous image.

Meet the Artist:
Shel Neymark, Shel Neymark Architectural Ceramics

"I have always loved architectural decoration. I also love clay, how it feels to work with, how it can be made into virtually any form, color, and texture. Making tile and architectural ceramic pieces evolved naturally for me as I pursued my life as an artist."

Shel Neymark, Shel Neymark Architectural Ceramics, *Doolittle Fountain*, mosaic, Botanical Gardens, Albuquerque, New Mexico. *Photograph by Herb Lotz*

Shel Neymark, Shel Neymark Architectural Ceramics, *Land of the Sun Fountain*, 8' diameter, 42" height. One of five ceramic fountains connected by decorated streams in Heritage Park, Artesia, New Mexico.

Shel Neymark, Shel Neymark Architectural Ceramics, detail of *Chili Tiles Stream*, 12" wide, installed in Heritage Park, Artesia, New Mexico.

Shel Neymark, *Cantaloupe Stream*, 12" wide, installed in Heritage Park, Artesia, New Mexico.

Shel Neymark, *Sheep Stream*, 12" wide, installed in Heritage Park, Artesia, New Mexico.

Sam Tubiolo, *Valle Grande and Jemez River*, bas-relief mural, 9'6" x 8'6", commissioned for the City/County Council Chambers, Los Alamos, New Mexico.

Frank Bosco, *Composition #2*, modified encaustic technique tile, 97 1/2" x 195". *Photograph by Les Helmers*

Linda Ellett, L'esperance Tile Works, decorative tile designed for Adirondack Trust Bank in Saratoga Spring, New York. 6" x 6" each.

Meet the Artist:
Pat Wehrman, Dodge Lane Potters Group

"*Morning Coffee* was commissioned by my hair dresser. She kept tabloids in her salon and I told her I was uncomfortable reading them for fear someone would see me, so she asked me to create someone to read with me. The idea was to make the kind of person that wouldn't bat an eye at the outrageous articles. Unfortunately the salon closed a couple of years ago, and the piece disappeared along with the hairdresser."

Pat Wehrman, Dodge Lane Potters Group, *Morning Coffee*, life-size wall mural.

149

Conclusion

For Love of Tile

There are so many ways that decorative tile can enrich our lives...in our homes, work places, and public spaces. One only has to imagine its myriad uses: a stone or brick fireplace holds our attention when a fire is blazing, whereas an exquisite tile fireplace surround is a riveting focal point any time of year; a plain kitchen backsplash comes alive when dotted with decorative tile insets; and a tiled table top always looks inviting, even when empty.

During the Tile Heritage Foundation's 1999 conference, we toured homes in Erie, Pennsylvania, which had many fine examples of tile from the early 1900s. I particularly remember the border tile in a bathroom which featured a whimsical but belligerent bullfrog staring at me from the shower stall. I couldn't help but imagine sharing my morning routine with this pudgy little fellow! I would certainly start each day with a smile!

I recall a story told to me by Elizabeth Grajales when she was installing her tiles in Pennsylvania Station in New York City. In a place where people typically avoid contact with strangers, a woman approached her, touched her arm, and looked straight into her eyes and said, "Thank you, thank you for giving me something beautiful to look at every day while I wait for my train!" I too have experienced a heartfelt response to my public artwork.

If you have the opportunity, I encourage you to find a place in your life for handmade decorative tile. It is a powerful way to express yourself and enliven your surroundings. Choose a design that touches your heart, and you will enjoy your creation for years to come.

Opposite page
Top: Elizabeth Murray, *Blooming* glass mosaic murals commissioned by the NY Metropolitan Transportation Authority/Arts for Transit, for 59th Street Station. Fabricated by Miotto Mosaics. *Photograph by Mike Kamber*

Deborah Brown, *Platform Diving*, glass mosaic mural series commissioned by the NY Metropolitan Transportation Authority/Arts for Transit, for the Houston Street Station. This mural measures 39" x 104", and was fabricated by Miotto Mosaics. *Photography by Adam Reich*

Acknowledgments

I would like to thank Joseph Taylor of the Tile Heritage Foundation for assistance with the historical information presented in Chapter Two.

I extend my appreciation to the following people for sharing their time, and offering insight into their respective fields of expertise. *See Index of Showrooms and Galleries for contact information.*

Sandra Bloodworth, MTA Arts for Transit
Leanne Croft, Leanne Croft Interiors
Robert Daniels, Tile Council of America
Nancy Epstein, Artistic Tile
Ruby Levesque
Bruce Levitt, Tiles - A Refined Selection
Jan MacLatchie, Artistic Tile
Diane Pilgrim
Akiko Uchida
Arnon Zadok, Ceramica Arnon
Adam Zayas, Moravian Pottery and Tile Works

I gratefully acknowledge each of the talented tile artists who contributed images of their work to create a dynamic visual survey of contemporary American art tile. See the Index of Tile Artists for contact information. I would especially like to thank the following tile artists for volunteering personal stories for the "Meet the Artist" sections.

Cristina Acosta
Kristina Baum
Véronique Blanchard
Frank Bosco
Linda Boston
Françoise Choveau

Lynda Curtis
Mahoko Dahte
Ginger Dunlap-Dietz
Nazaré Feliciano
Debra Felix
Michelle Griffoul
Norma and Kirsten Hanlon
Paul Lewing
Sally Mason
Keith Miller
Karim and Nawal Matowi
Shel Neymark
Ann and Edward Nocera
Linda Sheilds
Natalie Surving
Pat Wehrman
Paul Zelenka

Thank you to Tina Skinner, who challenged me with this project, and to Molly Higgins, my editor, for helping me through the process.

I am forever indebted to Judy Glasser, who first introduced me to clay, and continues to inspire me.

I extend my undying gratitude to Frank Giorgini, tile maker and educator extraordinaire, for being a true friend and guide in so many ways, for many years.

And heartfelt thanks to my husband, Eric, for his encouragement, and for putting up with all the sleepless nights, cereal dinners, and occasional whining he endured during the creation of this book.

Index of Tile Artists

Cristina Acosta
Cristina Acosta Art Studio
Bend, OR
Ph: 541-388-5157
Fax: 541-317-5586
cristina@CristinaAcosta.com
www.CristinaAcosta.com

Kim Adams
Custom-Made Tiles by Kim Adams
Boulder, CO
Ph: 303-442-7242
customtiles@hotmail.com

Nielsen Amon
Amon Art Tile
Brooklyn, NY
Ph/Fax: 718-768-5486

Antiquities Tile
Wiseman Spaulding Designs
Hampden, ME
Ph: 207-862-3513
Fax: 207-862-4513
antqtile@mint.net

Adriana Baler
Kensington, MD
Ph: 301-942-5985
adribaler@usa.net
www.adrianabalertiles.com

Kristina Baum
Gaithersburg, MD
Ph: 301-977-2155
shubunkin@erols.com
www.ShubunkinPottery.com

Liz Biddle
Croton-on-Hudson, NY
914-271-4666
breadbox@bestweb.net

Véronique Blanchard
Quilt Tiles by Véronique
New Hope, PA
Ph/Fax: 215-862-3734
vero@quilttiles.com
www.quilttiles.com

Frank Bosco
Jersey City, NJ
Ph: 201-432-9315
fbacarts@aol.com

Linda Boston
Waterford, MI
Ph/Fax: 248-681-5052
lboston888@mac.com

Deborah Brown
New York, NY
212-689-3657
EJPDRB@aol.com

Nancy Chevalier-Guido
Livonia, MI
NCGHandmadeTile@aol.com

Françoise Choveau
Rex Studio
Hereford, PA
Ph: 215-679-3801
rexstudio@hotmail.com

Craig Crawford
Tempest Tileworks
Jamestown, RI
Ph/Fax: 401-294-4303
ttst tiles@aol.com

Lynda Curtis
L. Curtis Designs
New Paltz, NY
lcschmoo@att.net

Mahoko Dahte
Cupertino, CA
Ph: 408-973-8597
Fax: 408-863-0447
mahoko@acga.net
www.acga.net/mahoko

Jeanie Daves
Clarksville, GA
Ph: 706-754-3254
wdaves@hemc.net

Steve de Perrot
Pots by de Perrot
Litty, PA
Ph: 717-627-6789
Fax: 717-627-2589
sdeperrot@supernet.net
www.potsbydeperrot.com

Susan Dunis
Dunis Studios
San Antonio, TX
210-497-5787
210-497-8987
dunis@wt.net
www.dunisstudios.com

Ginger Dunlap-Dietz
Eureka Studios
Syracuse, NY
Ph: 315-475-9565
Fax: 315-475-8003
gingerpots@aol.com
www.gingertiles.com

Michael F. Dupille
Seattle, WA
Ph: 206-248-2952
Fax: 206-622-4527
sunsetgrove@uswest.net

Linda Ellett
LÕesperance Tile
City Falls, NY
Ph: 518-884-2814
Fax: 518-885-4859
lestilewk1@aol.com

Stephen Fabrico
Bloomington, NY
Ph: 914-331-4760
Fax: 914-338-1356
budsandmud@aol.com

Nazare Feliciano
Chicago, IL

Debra Felix
Art Pottery & Tile
King of Prussia, PA
Ph: 610-345-9396
debmee7@aol.com

Frank Giorgini
Giorgini Studio
Freehold, NY
Ph: 518-634-2559
frank@udu.com
www.udu.com

Judy Glasser
Lynbrook, NY
Ph: 516-599-0210
jglasser_ceramic@hotmail.com

DeBorah Goletz
For Love of Mud
West Milford, NJ
Ph: 973-728-4889
Fax: 973-728-4298
dgoletz@earthlink.net
DecorativeArtTile.com

Kim Gore
Hand-Sculpted Tiles
Royal Oak, MI
Ph: 248-577-0568
kim@handsculptedtile.com

Elizabeth Grajales
Brooklyn, NY
Ph: 718-857-0729
EGrajales1@aol.com

Tia Grass
Modular Tile Art
East Grand Rapids, MI
Ph: 616-452-0424
tiagrass@juno.com

Michelle Griffoul
Michelle Griffoul Studios
Buellton, CA
Ph: 805-688-9631
Fax: 805-688-9965
Griffoul@aol.com
www.michellegriffoul.com

Katherine Hackl
Swan Street Studio
Lambertville, NJ
Ph: 609-397-9073
Fax: 609-397-7570

Norma & Kristen Hanlon
Fresh Fish Ceramic Tiles
Minneapolis, MN
Ph: 612-824-3325
Fax: 612-824-1235
norma@freshfishtiles.com
kristen@freshfishtiles.com
www.freshfishtiles.com

Joan Rothchild Hardin
New York, NY
Ph: 212-966-9433
Fax: 212-431-9196
joan@hardintiles.com
www.hardintiles.com

Nancy Holcomb
Creative Design Tiles
Little Torch Key, FL
(305) 872-1155
Nancycdt@aol.com
www.creativedesigntiles@aol.com

Tania Huusko
Brittany & Coggs
Dover, NH
Ph: 603-742-5122
Fax: 603-742-5174

Susan Kemenyffy
Raku Place
McKean, PA
Ph: 814-734-4421
Fax: 814-734-4736
raku@erie.net

Eui-Kyung Lee
New York, NY
Ph: 212-288-4357
eklee_ny@yahoo.com
www.claywall.com

Pedro Leitao
Solar Antique Tiles
New York, NY
Ph: 212-755-2403
Fax: 212-980-2649
pleitao@aol.com
www.solarantiquetiles.com

Ruby Levesque
Amon Art Tile
Brooklyn, NY
Ph/Fax: 718-768-5486
rubylevesque@yahoo.com

Bev Leviner
Hilltop Studio
Reading, PA
Ph: 610-926-3225
bml3@psu.edu

Paul Lewing
Seattle, WA
Ph: 206-547-6591
pjlewing@worldnet.att.net

Margaret Licha
Margaret Licha Designs
Orangevale, CA
Ph/Fax: 916-988-0239
rubytile@yahoo.com
margaretlichatile.com

Sally Mason
Black Dog Clayworks
Tucson, AZ
Ph/Fax: 520-822-1321
blackdogclay@cs.com

Carolin Meier
California Clay
Oakland, CA
Ph: 510-655-1466
carolin@calclay.com
www.calclay.com

Meredith Art Tile
a division of Ironrock Capital, Inc.
Canton, OH
Ph: 330-1656
Fax: 330-484-9380
grenkert@meredithcollection.com
www.meredithtile.com

Keith Miller
Sugar Lake Pottery
Pittsboro, NC
Ph: 919-542-3905
sugarlake@mindspring.com
www.sugarlakepottery.com

Moravian Pottery & Tileworks
Doylestown, PA
Ph: 215-345-6722
www.mercermuseum.org

Karim & Nawal Motawi
Motawi Tileworks
Ann Arbor, MI
Ph: 734-213-0017
motawi@motawi.com
www.motawi.com

Shel Neymark
Embudo, NM
Ph/Fax: 505-579-4432
lizshel@cybermesa.com

Anne & Edward Nocera
Nocera Art Tile Co.
Milanville, PA
Ph: 570-729-7946
Fax: 570-729-7317
article@voicenet.com
www.art-tile.com

Mark Oliver
Farmingdale, NJ
Ph/Fax: 732-919-3701
wearei@netzero.net
www.artofmark.com

Phyllis Pacin
Oakland, CA
Ph: 510-530-7059
ppacin@yahoo.com

Kristin & Steven Powers
Trikeenan Tileworks, Inc.
Keene, NH
Ph: 603-352-4299
Fax: 352-9843
trikeenan@webryders.com
www.trikeenan.com

Angelica Pozo
Cleveland, OH
Ph: 216-241-6936
Fax: 216-861-6566
angelicapozo@earthlink.net

Celine Quemere
Quemere International
Port Chester, NY
Ph: 914-934-8366
Fax: 914-934-8401

Phil Raskin
North Prairie Tileworks
Minneapolis, MN
Ph: 612-871-3421
information@handmadetile.com
www.handmadetile.com

Sergio Salgado
Capistrano Beach, CA
Ph: 240-5157

Alison Sawyer
BayFire Studios
Boulder, CO
Ph: 303-443-6769
bayfirestd@aol.com

Donna J. Schuurhuis
Schuurhuis Studio
Silverthorne, CO
Ph: 970-262-1443
Fax: 970-262-6193
leonard@colorado.net

Linda Shields
Atherton Tile Company
San Carlos, CA
Ph: 888-393-8453
Fax: 650-595-3322
lshields@athertontile.com
www.athertontile.com

Laura Shprentz
Port Chester, NY
Ph: 914-939-6639

Bonnie Smith
Kingston, NY
Ph: 914-340-8055

Sonoma Tilemakers
Windsor, CA
Ph: 707-837-8177
Fax: 707-837-9472
info@sonomatilemakers.com
www. sonomatilemakers.com

Nancy Saragoulis
Hilltop Studio
Reading, PA
Ph: 610-926-3225

Laura Lyn Stern
Scuptural Designs
Philadelphia, PA
Ph/Fax: 215-765-1646
lalystern@aol.com

Natalie & Richard Surving
Middletown, NY
Ph: 800-768-4954
Fax: 845-355-1517
surving@warwick.net
www.surving.com

Delia & Marie Glasse Tapp
Tile Restoration Center
Seattle, WA
Ph: 206-633-4866
Fax: 206-633-3489
trc@wolfenet.com

Chris Troy
Seneca, SC
Ph: 864-985-1096
Fax: 864-882-1095
cttroy@innova.net

Penny Truitt
Santa Fe, NM
Ph: 505-466-1656
Rosedale, VA
Ph: 540-873-4228

Sam Tubiolo
Sacramento, CA
Ph: 916-442-1941
ChTuMa@aol.com

Rosalyn Tyge
Tygetile Art
Traverse City, MI
Ph: 231-943-8073
Fax: 248-671-0360
tygetile@northlink.net

Holly P. Walker
Belden, MS
Ph: 662-841-0183
hollypots@yahoo.com

Pat Wehrman
Dodge Lane Potters Group
Sonora, CA
Ph: 209-532-9124
Fax: 209-532-7713
tile@dlpg.com
www.dlpg.com

Diane Winters
Winters Tileworks
Berkeley, CA
Ph: 510-533-7624
diane@winterstileworks.com
www.winterstileworks.com

Paul Zelenka
Unicorn Studio
Park City, UT
Ph: 435-649-3611
Fax: 435-649-7686

Index of Showrooms & Galleries

Alabama

Ceramic Harmony
11317 Memorial Pkwy SW
Huntsville, AL 35803
Ph: 256-883-1204

International Tile & Stone
100 Commerce Ct
Pelham, AL 35124
Ph: 205-987-3617

Arizona

Craftsman Court Ceramics, Inc
4169 North Craftsman Ct
Scottsdale, AZ 85251
Ph: 480-970-6611

Old Town Pot Shop
186 North Meyer Ave
Tucson, AZ 85701
Ph: 520-620-1725

Tile West
3757 East Broadway
Phoenix, AZ 85040
Ph: 602-437-4400

Tile West
14525 North 79th St
Scottsdale, AZ 85260
Ph: 480-922-8801

Tile West
1665 East 18th St #123
Tucson, AZ 85719
Ph: 520-620-1665

California

A Gallery Fine Art
73-956 El Paseo
Palm Desert, CA 92260
Ph: 760-346-8885

Alexis Deutsch Fine Art
2444 Wilshire Blvd, #508
Santa Monica, CA 90403
Ph: 310-315-5400

Andrea Schwartz Gallery
333 Bryant St, Suite 180
San Francisco, CA 94107
Ph: 415-495-2090

Ann Sacks Tile & Stone Inc
2 Henry Adams, Suite 125
San Francisco, CA 94103
Ph: 415-252-5889

Anne Saunders Gallery
18381 Main St
Jamestown, CA 95327
Ph: 209-984-4421

Architectural Amenities
6 South Central Ct
Stockton, CA 95204
Ph: 209-547-0480

The Art Collector
4151 Taylor St
San Diego, CA 92110
Ph: 619-299-3232

Art Concepts
2121 N Californial Blvd # 305
Walnut Creek, CA 94596
Ph: 925-930-0157

Bolivar
One West California Blvd
Suite 111
Pasadena, CA 91105
Ph: 626-449-8453

Ceramic Tile Supply
180 Roymar Rd #A
Oceanside, CA 92054
Ph: 760-433-3555

Chic Tile
1590 Industrial Way
Redwood City, CA 94063
Ph: 650-366-2442

Classic Tile & Design
860 Pacific Coast Highway
Hermosa Beach, CA 90254
Ph: 310-376-8024

CTW Designs
10 Hamilton Drive
Novato, CA 94949
Ph: 415-883-8861

Decorative Tile & Bath
18416 Ventura Blvd
Tarzana, CA 91356
Ph: 818-344-3536

Design Showcase
1758 Industrial Way, #208
Napa, CA 94558
Ph: 707-255-7115

Dorthy's Ceramic Tile
925 Carver Rd
Modesto, CA 95350
Ph: 209-521-9395

European Tile Art
6440 Lusk Blvd, Suite D-107
San Diego, CA 92121
Ph: 858-452-5090

Foothills Tile & Stone Co
2272 East Walnut St
Pasadena, CA 91107
Ph: 626-396-9620

Home Concepts Truckee-Tahoe
10242 Church St
Truckee, CA 96160
Ph: 530-587-9211

International Bath & Tile
7177 Convoy Ct, Suite A
San Diego, CA 92111
Ph: 858-268-3723

Italics Ceramic Tile
901 East Francisco Blvd E
San Rafael, CA 94101
Ph: 415-451-6150

Mission Tile West
1207 Fourth St
Santa Monica, CA 90403
Ph: 310-434-9697

Mission Tile West
853 Mission St
South Pasadena, CA 91030
Ph: 626-799-4595

Natural Stone Design Gallery
5691-A Power Inn Rd
Sacramento, CA 95824
Ph: 916-387-6207

N S Ceramic
401 East Carrillo St - #A1
Santa Barbara, CA 93101
Ph: 805-962-1422

Stone & Ceramic Surfaces
5381 Commercial Drive
Huntington Beach, CA 92649
Ph: 714-894-8453

Surface Concepts
26061 Merit Circle, Suite 105
Laguna Hills, CA 92653
Ph: 949-348-1088

Susan Street Fine Art Gallery
444 S Cedros Ave, # 100
Solana Beach, CA 92075
Ph: 619-793-4442

Tile & Plumbing Gallery
19431 Beach Blvd
Huntington Beach, CA 92648
Ph: 714-536-8722

Tile Source
949 Industrial Ave
Palo Alto, CA 94303
Ph: 650-424-8672

Tile & Stone Concepts
1505 Francisco Blvd East
San Rafael, CA 94901
Ph: 415-457-9422

Tile Town
2235 North Main St
Walnut Creek, CA 94596
Ph: 925-939-4884

Tugend Tile
1644 Abbott Kinney Blvd
Venice, CA 90291
Ph: 310-399-0130

Victory Tile & Marble Inc
68796 Perez Rd
Cathedral City, CA 92234
Ph: 760-321-6000

Walker Zanger
350 Clinton Street Suite A
Costa Mesa, CA
Ph: 714-546-3671

Walker Zanger
8901 Bradley Ave
Sun Valley, CA 91352
Ph: 818-504-0235

Walker Zanger
8750 Melrose Ave
West Hollywood, CA 90069
Ph: 310-659-1234

Walls Alive
1754C Junction Ave
San Jose, CA 95112
Ph: 408-436-8131

Colorado

Decorative Materials Intl, Ltd.
40 Sunset Drive #10A
Basalt, CO 81621
Ph: 970-927-0700

Decorative Materials Intl, Ltd.
595 South Broadway, #108W
Denver, CO 80209
Ph: 303-722-1333

Connecticut

Ceramic Design, Ltd.
29 Bruce Park Ave
Greenwich, CT 06830
Ph: 203-869-8800

Country Floors
12 East Putnam Avenue
Greenwich CT, 06830
Ph: 203-862-9900

Design Works
855 Middlesex Trnpk
Old Saybrook, CT 06475
Ph: 860-388-5366

Port America Design Ctr
425 Post Rd East
Westport, CT 06880
Ph: 203-226-2533

Sasso Tile Co.
55 Dogburn Ext.
West Haven, CT 06516
Ph: 203-795-9741

Westport Tile & Design
175 Post Rd West
Westport, CT 06880
Ph: 203-454-0032

Wirth-Salander Tile Studio
132 North Washington St #C
South Norwalk, CT 06854
Ph: 203-852-9449

Delaware

Charles Taylor & Sons, Inc
2870 Creek Rd
Yorklyn, DE 19736
Ph: 302-234-4700

Tile & Stoneworks Ltd
2892 Creek Rd #B3
Yorklyn, DE 19736
Ph: 302-234-9500

Florida

Ceramic Matrix of Florida, Inc
3800 N.E. Second Ave
Miami, FL 33137
Ph: 305-573-5997

Ceramic Matrix
3500 45th St #11
Suite 16
West Palm Beach, FL 33407
Ph: 561-681-6810

Harmony Isle
902 NE 19th Ave
Fort Lauderdale, FL 33304
Ph: 954-527-2880

International Tile & Stone
114 South Palafox Place
Pensacola, FL 32501
Ph: 850-429-0500

Kennedy Gallery
1000 Duval St
Key West, FL 33040
Ph: 305-294-5997

Southwest Tile & Design, Inc
4034 N Washington Blvd #9
Sarasota, FL 34234
Ph: 941-355-8373

Suncoast Tile & Marble Design
320 West Bay Drive
Largo, FL 33770
Ph: 727-585-6914

Tile Market of Naples Inc
1170 Third St South #B110
Naples, FL 34102
Ph: 941-261-9008

Tile Market
1221 First St
Sarasota, FL 34236
Ph: 941-365-2356

Tile Market
834 Orange Ave
Winter Park, FL 32789
Ph: 407-628-4322

Tile Market Treasure Coast
320 South Federal Highway
Stuart, FL 34994
Ph: 561-283-2125

Traditions in Tile
7660 Phillips Highway, Suite 8
Jacksonville, FL 33256
Ph: 904-739-7386

Georgia

The Art-Full Barn
679 Grant St
Clarkesville, GA 30523
Ph: 706-754-1247

Byrdhouse Design Ctr, Ltd.
2010 Abercorn St (Sisters Ct)
Savannah, GA 31401
Ph: 912-447-6720

Traditions in Tile
1495 Hembree Rd
Roswell, GA 30076
Ph: 770-343-9104

Westchester Marble & Granite
791 Miami Circle N.E.
Atlanta, GA 30324
Ph: 404-365-9991

Hawaii

Trans-Pacific Design
65-1235 Opelo Rd #8
Kamuela, Hawaii 96743
Ph: 808-885-5587

Illinois

The Fine Line
209 West Illinois St
Chicago, IL 60610
Ph: 312-670-0300

Tile Concepts of Hinsdale
212 East Chicago Ave
Westmont, IL 60559
Ph: 630-920-0949

Iowa

RBC Iowa
2001 NW 92nd Ct
Clive, IA 50325
Ph: 515-224-1200

Kansas

Itnl Materials/Country Floors
4691 Indian Creek Pkwy
Shawnee Mission, KS 66207
Ph: 913-383-3383

Maryland

Annapolis Accents, Inc
100 Annapolis St, Suite B
Annapolis, MD 21401
Ph: 410-263-4700

Chesapeake Tile & Marble, Inc
45 Gwynns Mill Ct
Owing Mills, MD 21117
Ph: 410-363-7363

Massachusetts

Cape Cod Tileworks
705 Main St
Harwich, MA 02645
Ph: 508-432-7346

Leanne Croft Interiors
25 Oriole Drive
Andover, MA 01810
Ph: 978-470-2261

Once Upon A Tile
12 Westminster St
Fitchberg, MA 01420
Ph: 978-345-8343

Roma Tile
400 Arsenal St
Watertown, MA 02472
Ph: 617-926-5800

Terra Cotta II
117 Teapelo Rd
Belmont, MA 02178
Ph: 617-489-4424

Tiles-A Refined Selection Inc
Boston Design Centre
1 Design Centre Place
Boston, MA 02210
Ph: 617-357-5522

Upstairs Downstairs Tile
6 Great Rd Rt 2A
Acton, MA 01720
Ph: 978-369-3620

Michigan

Andy Sharkey Gallery Inc
510 Washington Ave
Royal Oak, MI 48067
Ph: 248-546-6770

Ann Arbor Art Center
117 West Liberty
Ann Arbor, MI 48104
Ph: 734-994-8004

Ariana Gallery
119 South Main St
Royal Oak, MI 48073
Ph: 248-546-8810

Ariel's Enchanted Garden
23712 Gratiot
Eastpointe, MI 48021
Ph: 810-775-2820

Biddle Gallery
2840 Biddle Ave
Wyandotte, MI 48192
Ph: 734-281-4779

Dancing Eye Gallery
150 N Center St
Northville, MI 48167
Ph: 248-449-7086

Jules Furniture Inc
306 South Main St
Ann Arbor, MI 48104
Ph: 734-332-3408

Now & Then Gallery
136 Butler St
Saugatuck, MI 49453
Ph: 616-857-3036

Painted Bird
216 St. Joseph Ave.
Suttons Bay, MI 49682
Ph: 231-271-3050

Pewabic Pottery
10125 E. Jefferson Ave
Detroit MI 48214
Ph: 313-822-0954

Tvedten Fine Art Gallery
284 East Third St
P.O. Box 654
Harbor Springs, MI 49740
Ph: 231-526-2299

Virginia Tile Co
24404 Indoplex Circle
Farmington Hills, MI 48335
Ph: 248-476-7850

Virginia Tile Co
3440 Broadmoor SE
Grand Rapids, MI 49512
Ph: 616-942-6200

Virginia Tile Co
7689 Nineteen Mile Rd
Sterling Heights, MI 48314
Ph: 810-254-4960

Virginia Tile Co
1700 Stutz Drive, #22
Troy, MI 48084
Ph: 248-649-4422

Minnesota

Fantasia Showrooms
275 Market St, #102
Minneapolis, MN 55405
Ph: 612-338-5811

Nebraska

RBC Omaha
9333 H. Ct
Omaha, NE 68127
Ph: 402-331-0665

Nevada

Aurora Marble & Stone
4999 Aircenter Crl, Suite 104
Reno, NV 89502
Ph: 775-829-1177

European Bath & Kitchen
4050 South Decatur Blvd
Las Vegas, NV 89114
Ph: 702-873-8600

R M Tile & Stone
804 Packer Way
Sparks, NV 89431
Ph: 775-331-8048

New Jersey

A W Eurostile
41 Newman Springs Rd
Shrewsbury, NJ 07702
Ph: 732-530-9186

Abbot Tile
303 US Route 22E
Green Brook, NJ 08812
Ph: 732-968-0018

Artistic Tile Inc.
727 Route 17 South
Paramus, NJ 07652
Ph: 201-670-6100

Artistic Tile Inc
777 Broad St
Shrewsbury, NJ 07739
Ph: 732-212-1616

Bergen Brick, Stone, Tile
685 Wykoff Ave
Wykoff, NJ 07481
Ph: 210-981-0088

Charles Tiles Inc
760 Country Rt 523
Stockton, NJ 08559
Ph: 609-397-0330

Mediterranean Tile & Marble
461 Route 46 W-Crown Plaza
Fairfield, NJ 07004
Ph: 973-808-1267

Terra Designs, Inc
49B Route 202 South
Far Hills, NJ 07931
Ph: 908-234-0440

W D Virtue Tile Co
160 Broad St
Summit, NJ 07901
Ph: 908-273-6936

New Mexico

Counterpoint Tile
320 Sandoval
Santa Fe, NM 87501
Ph: 505-982-1247

New York

Alan Court & Associates Inc
36 Park Place
East Hampton, NY 11937
Ph: 631-324-7497

Ann Sacks Tile & Stone
5 East 16th St
New York, NY 10003
Ph: 800-377-TILE

Artistic Tile Inc
79 Fifth Ave
New York, NY 10003
Ph: 212-727-9331

Artistic Tile Inc
65 Tarrytown Rd
White Plains, NY 10607
Ph: 914-422-0041

Brooklyn Artisans Gallery
221 Court St #A
Brooklyn, NY 11201
Ph: 718-330-0343

Ceramica Arnon
134 West 20th St
New York, NY 10011
Ph: 212-807-0876

Country Floors
15 East 16th St
New York, NY 10003
Ph: 212-627-8300

Fancy Fixtures
475 Port Washington Blvd
Port Washington, NY 11050
Ph: 516-767-3500

Gary Baydal Tile Industries Inc
1070 Bay St
Staten Island, NY 10305
Ph: 718-727-5566

New Main Street Gallery
398 Main Street
Catskill, NY 12414
Ph: 518-943-3400

J George Tile & Stone
150 East 58th St, 8A
New York, NY 10155
Ph: 212-751-7222

Shelly Tile Ltd.
979 Third Ave, #819
New York, NY 10022
Ph: 212-832-2255

Stone Age
10 Purchase St
Rye, NY 10580
Ph: 914-921-0697

Stoneworks Tile & Bath
295 Rockaway Trnpk
Lawrence, NY 11559
Ph: 516-239-9730

Tile Barn Inc/Rico Tile Co
17 East Jericho Trnpk
Huntington Station, NY 11746
Ph: 631-673-5804

Tiles-A Refined Selection
227 East 59th St
New York, NY 10022
Ph: 212-813-9391

Tiles-A Refined Selection
42 West 15th St
New York, NY 10011
Ph: 212-255-4450

The Tile Studio
#1 Lansdowne Ave
Merrick, NY 11566
Ph: 516-623-2600

Urban Archaeology
239 East 58th St
New York, NY 10022
Ph: 212-371-4646

Urban Archaeology
143 Franklin St
New York, NY 10013
Ph: 212-431-4646

Watercross Plumbing Gallery
Mt. Kisco Design Center
193 North Main St
Mt. Kisco, NY 10549
Ph: 914-242-9011

North Carolina

Laufen Intl
3402 South Blvd
Charlotte, NC 28209
Ph: 704-527-1355

Ohio

Surface Style
6650 Busch Blvd
Columbus, OH 43229
Ph: 614-228-6990

Thomas Brick Co
27750 Chagin Blvd
Cleveland, OH 44122
Ph: 216-831-9116

Thomas Brick Co West
The Ohio Building Mart
975 Crocker Rd
Westlake, OH 44145
Ph: 440-892-9400

Oregon

Ann Sacks Tile & Stone Inc
1210 SE Grand Ave
Portland, OR 97214
Ph: 503-233-0611

The Tile Gallery
1416 West 7th
Eugene, OR 97402
Ph: 541-342-8288

United Tile
3435 S.E. 17th Ave
Portland, OR 97202
Ph: 503-231-4958

West Valley Ceramic Tile Co
20001 SW Tualatin Valley Hwy
Beaverton, OR 97007
Ph: 503-649-7825

Pennsylvania

Clay Studio
139 N 2nd St
Philadelphia, PA
Ph: 215-925-3453

Devon Tile Design Studio
111 East Lancaster Ave
Devon, PA 19333
Ph: 610-687-3368

Joanne Hudson Assoc Ltd
2400 Market St #310
Suite 310
Philadelphia, PA 19103
Ph: 215-568-5501

Moravian Pottery & Tile Works
130 Swamp Rd (Rt 313)
Doylestown, PA 18901
Ph: 215-345-6722

Show of Hands
1006 Pine St
Philadelphia, PA
Ph: 215-592-4010

Tileology
245 Centerville Rd
Lancaster, PA 17603
Ph: 717-290-7444

Oregon

Ann Sacks Tile & Stone Inc
1210 SE Grand Ave
Portland, OR 97214
Ph: 503-233-0611

Rhode Island

Newport Tile & Marble
1151 Aquidneck Ave
Middletown, RI 02842
Ph: 401-846-9911

South Carolina

The Arts Co
125 North Townville St
Seneca, SC 29678
Ph: 864-882-0840

South Carolina Artisans Center
334 Wichman St
Walterboro, S.C. 29488
Ph: 843-549-0011

Tennesse

Traditions in Tile
2548 Bransford Ave
Nashville, TN 37204
Ph: 888-262-9669

Venice Tile & Marble
3665 South Perkins, Suite #1
Memphis, TN 38118
Ph: 901-547-9770

Texas

Antique Floors Inc
1221 Dragon St
Dallas, TX 75207
Ph: 214-760-9330

Architectural Design Resource
5120 Woodway, Suite 115
Houston, TX 77056
Ph: 713-877-8366

Architerra Austin
1701 Evergreen Ave #2
Austin, TX 78704
Ph: 512-441-8062

French-Brown Floors
7007 Greenville Ave
Dallas, TX 75231
Ph: 214-363-4341

Palmer Todd, Inc
203 West Rhapsody Dr
San Antonio, TX 87216
Ph: 210-341-3396

Walker Zanger
7055 Old Katy Rd
Houston, TX 77024
Ph: 713-880-9292

Utah

Domestic-Import Tile & Marble
3650 South 300 West
Salt Lake City, Utah 84115
Ph: 801-262-3033

Vermont

Down East Tile
723 Sylvan Park Rd
Stowe, VT 05672
Ph: 802-253-7001

Green Mountain Tile Dstrs
RR #2 Box 1136 Route 7A
Harwood Hill
Bennington, VT 05201
Ph: 802-447-3393

Virginia

Ademas
816 North Fairfax St
Alexandria, VA 22314
Ph: 703-549-7806

Washington

Ann Sacks Tile & Stone
115 Stewart Ave
Seattle, WA 98101
Ph: 206-441-8917

Lutz Tile
445 East Main St
Puyallup, WA 98372
Ph: 253-840-5011

Norberry Tile
207 Second Ave South
Seattle, WA 98104
Ph: 206-343-9916

The Tile Store
5373 Guide Meridian #C4
Bellingham, WA 98226
Ph: 360-398-1186

United Tile
3001 East Valley Rd
Renton, WA 98055
Ph: 425-251-5390

Wisconsin

Ann Sacks Tile & Stone
765 Woodlake Rd #1
Kohler, WI 53044
Ph: 414-452-7250

Index of Organizations

National Council on Education
for the Ceramic Arts (NCECA)
P.O. Box 777
Erie, CO 80516-0777

Tile Council of America
100 Clemson Research Blvd
Anderson, SC 29625
Ph: 864-646-8453

Tile Heritage Foundation
P.O. Box 1850
Healdsburg, CA 95448
Ph: 707-431-8453
www.tileheritage.org
foundation@tileheritage.org